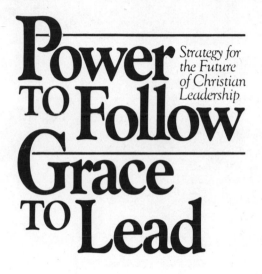

Power
TO Follow
Grace
TO Lead

Strategy for
the Future
of Christian
Leadership

Books by DAVID L. MCKENNA

Mark (in the Communicator's Commentary Series)
Job (in the Communicator's Commentary Series)
The Psychology of Jesus
The Whisper of His Grace
Renewing Our Ministry

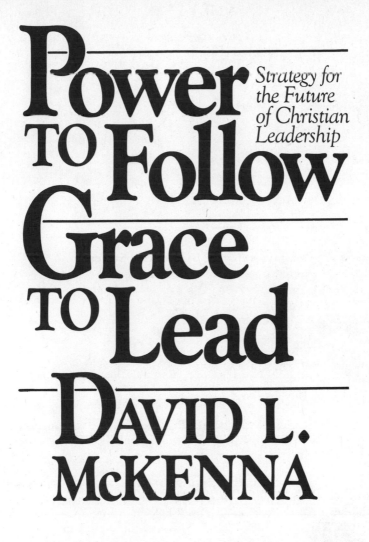

Power to Follow Grace to Lead

Strategy for the Future of Christian Leadership

DAVID L. McKENNA

WORD PUBLISHING
Dallas · London · Sydney · Singapore

Library of Congress Cataloging-in-Publication Data

McKenna, David L. (David Loren), 1929–
    Power to follow, grace to lead.

    Bibliography: p.
    1. Christian leadership. I. Title.
BV652.1.M34   1989   262'.1   88-28008
ISBN   0-8499-0674-1

Contents

1

Prologue:
Who Will Lead Us?

WANTED:

A new generation of Christian leaders for the twenty-first century. Must be willing to embody Christ and empower others. All interested parties are urged to apply.

Christian leadership in the secular society is at a crossroads. Behind us is the checkered history of the twentieth century. Theological division opened the century, cultural Christianity absorbed the middle years and an aborted "Great Awakening" has blurred the closing years. Ahead of us is the twenty-first century with its options of threat and opportunity. Whether Christians will retreat because of threats or seize the opportunities is an open question.

Without discounting the movement of the Holy Spirit or the surprises of God, the leaders we choose today will set the pace for the way we will go. Our particular concern is for Christians who are called to lead in the secular setting. They are the "leaven" which activates kingdom principles in the rising loaf of our culture and the "salt" which preserves those principles in a changing social climate. Whether they are described as "missionaries without portfolio" or the "third force" between the church and the world, we count on them for the future. Especially on the threshold of the twenty-first century, each of us is asking,

- Who will lead us?
- What kind of leadership do we need?
- How are Christian leaders different?

So, the search is on. A new generation of leaders is needed to go before us into the twenty-first century. Not that our current leaders of the twentieth century have failed us. Rather, it is time for them to take their leave. While revering their role as our elder statesmen and seeking the wisdom of their counsel, we still need new energy and new perspective for the new millennium. New energy is needed to cope with the speed and intensity of the challenges before us. New perspective is needed to deal with the complexity and ambiguity of our changing times.

If only our past leaders had nurtured this new generation. Almost too late, it seems, we are discovering our larger responsibility for mentoring future leaders and our specific task of preparing our successors. Consequently, on the threshold of the new millennium, we must begin with an open question.

Who Will Lead Us?

The speaker who posed the question was addressing a meeting of prominent Christian leaders, both clergy and laity. Yet his question hung suspended in the air. Only the silence spoke. Either the assembled Christian leaders assumed they were the answer or they had never considered the question.

Whatever the reason for their silence, the speaker went on to note that we are living in a "privileged time" in the closing years of the twentieth century just as our forefathers lived in a "privileged time" one hundred years ago. They, however, were only anticipating a new century. We are coming into a new millennium. Of course, there is no magic in a new millennium. The time will come with just another second ticking off the clock like New Year's Eve on Times Square. Yet, there is something different when centuries change and new millennia arrive. Our natural tendency is to pause, reflect upon the past and look forward to the future.

One hundred years ago, when our forefathers stood on the threshold of the twentieth century, their anticipation reached euphoric proportions. Despite the wounds of Civil War, the incipient threats of industrialization and urbanization, the economic split between rich and poor, the potential clash with migrant minorities, the rising expectations for education and the inevitable pull from isolation into world affairs, they fashioned the "American dream" of social equality, economic opportunity, educational accessibility, moral stability and world peace. To celebrate their dream, they danced their way through the last decade of the nineteenth century to the foot-tapping tunes and carefree styles of the "Gay '90s." Furthermore, to endow their dream for the twentieth century with theological credibility, they founded *The Christian Century* magazine in 1902 as the house organ for liberal Christianity and foresaw its purpose to chronicle the Second Coming brought about by the social gospel.

The great American dream of our forefathers got mugged by reality in the twentieth century. Even though *The Christian Century* magazine still exists, it limps along with a circulation of 30,000 while *Christianity Today,* an evangelical journal founded in 1956, is the undisputed leader of religious journals with a total circulation upwards of 180,000. In quick defense, we may argue that the realism is good for us. Perhaps so, but realism weighted down by fear can be deadening.

A 1988 Gallup poll, one of the most intensive ever taken, revealed an underlying *fear among the American people* as we approach the twenty-first century. Despite the economic successes of the 1980s which gave Americans a short-term sense of well-being, the majority of us fears the collapse of our national economy before the turn of the century due to foreign competition.

Even more significantly, the Gallup poll draws a direct connection between our fear of the future and our lack of confidence in the caliber of leaders who are coming on the scene. Not only do we foresee circumstances which outstrip the competence of our rising leaders, but we also doubt their credibility to hold the course when the needle of our moral compass is swinging wildly back and forth from pole to pole.

The truth comes home. One hundred years ago, we dreamed of a new century and danced through the "Gay '90s." Today, we have the appearance of prosperity with ashes in our mouth. We dread the "Grim '90s" and we dare not dream of the new millennium.

Some place between the euphoria of our forefathers and our current fear of the future, we need realistic optimism. This is what the speaker had in mind when he reminded Christian leaders that we are living in a "privileged time." Realistic optimism shows us that we *can* anticipate a new century and a new millennium.

Despite localized rumbles of revolution and skirmishes of war, our world is at peace. Despite insufferable pockets of poverty, we have in our hands the economic resources to feed the hungry and house the homeless. Despite unnecessary ignorance over the globe, we have the techniques and the technology for teaching all nations. Despite the threat of a world-wide epidemic of AIDS, we are rallying with compassion for its victims and reassessing absolute values in sexual morality. Despite the feverish attempts of dictators to remain in power, the thrusts for democratic freedom cannot be stifled. Despite the shadows of darkest evil, we see the signs of spiritual resurgence in every corner of the world.

The speaker was right. This is a "privileged time" in which our opportunities outweigh our threats. Leadership will make the difference. With the privilege of pausing to reflect upon our past and anticipate our future, we need leaders who will see the vision, state the mission and set the tone that will raise the sights and lift the spirits of our people.

What Kind of Leaders Do We Need?

Whenever we ask, "Who will lead us?" a companion question immediately follows, "What kind of leaders do we need?" Today, the question has suspicious overtones. *Confidence* in our leaders has been severely shaken by events of recent years. The 1960s started out with blind confidence in the charisma of the Kennedys. Who can ever forget the parody of Washington, D.C. as the "grim world of the brothers wonderful?" Or who can ever forget the bright-eyed, silver-tongued and rosy-cheeked young mayors at the beginning of the 1960s who convinced us that they could transform urban blight into shining cities?

By the end of the decade, however, our leaders had lost legitimacy. Dallas, Selma, Berkeley, My Lai, Grant Park, Twelfth Street and Woodstock were symbols of their failure. At least in the minds of the young, the right to lead was no longer a "given." The legitimacy of leadership had to be earned again and again. As we approach the twenty-first century, the young people of the 1960s have grown up, but their attitude toward leadership is a legacy that persists. Confidence has no carryover from day to day.

If the foundation for the legitimacy of leadership crumbled in the 1960s, the structure for *credibility* disintegrated in the 1970s. Watergate, of course, had a ripple effect throughout all leadership ranks. Distrust overrode confidence and public scrutiny replaced blind loyalty. Consequently, the character flaws of past leaders, which we overlooked or forgave, are now exposed in full color and sordid detail for the leaders of today. Whether in government, business, education or religion, to serve as a leader is to be under the microscopic scrutiny of the public eye.

Credibility of leadership is no longer taken for granted. Position no longer assures respect. Leaders of the twenty-first century will have to overcome the lengthening shadows and the lingering doubts which now follow prominent people in every sector of our society. "Integrity" is the standard, "accountability" is the demand and "credibility" is the judgment. None will be taken for granted.

With confidence in our leadership shaken in the '60s and credibility undermined in the '70s, it is no surprise to find the *competence* of our leaders questioned in the 1980s. In national politics, for instance, pundits write with pens dipped in sarcasm, "we are hip-deep in pygmies." In international affairs, a similar sound is echoed in judgment upon our diplomatic leadership, "We have nuclear giants and ethical dwarfs." Consequently, we find ourselves retreating on our expectations for leadership. Overwhelmed by technical complexity, media fluff and moral ambiguity, we settle for "image" over "issues" and "style" over "substance." At best, leadership for the future is a shot in the dark.

How are Christian Leaders Different?

Christian leaders have been caught in the backwash of these happenings. Whether a leader is in a Christian or secular setting, there is no difference. *Confidence* must be earned every day; *credibility* is no longer automatic; and *competence* is an open question. These issues, however, are only surface indicators of a deeper problem. With the undermining of authority, the erosion of morality and the loss of the sacred in society, the leverage for Christian leadership has been reduced to the narrowest of margins. Add to these changes the troubles in our primary institutions—the home, church and school. Leaders, whether secular or Christian, are not loners. They must have followers to be effective and institutions to be efficient. Christian leaders, in particular, are dependent upon the corporate and communal Body of Christ as represented in the home, the church and the school. Radical individualism, a characteristic of our time, is a mortal enemy of Christian leadership.

Not all the blame for the crises of confidence, credibility and competence in Christian leadership can be placed upon external or secular circumstances. In too many instances, Christian leaders have suffered from self-inflicted wounds. Caught up in the spiral of secular success and celebrity status, highly visible Christian leaders have burned out, dropped out and fallen into scandal. More subtle and less spectacular, however, has been the easy accommodation with the influence and affluence of Western culture. One needs only to read *The Coming of the Third Church* by Walbert Buhlmann to realize how far the Second Church of the West has strayed from the apostolic vitality surging through the Third Church movements in the developing nations south of the equator.

Most telling is the testimony of a Rumanian pastor who was set free from prison and torture behind the iron curtain. Sensing the lack of spiritual depth in the Western Church, he said that his suffering now ". . . consisted in his longing for the indescribable beauty of his persecuted Church, following Christ in poverty and nakedness."[1] We who are Christian leaders in the Western Church must share some responsibility for the loss of confidence, credibility and competence which has cast a long shadow over our image.

How can we restore the confidence, credibility and competence of Christian leadership for the twenty-first century? The need for an answer to the question is best expressed in the popular market for books on Christian leadership. Examples are Fred Smith's *Learning to Lead,* Ted Engstrom's *Integrity,* Harold Myra's *Leaders,* James Johnson's *Excellence* and Eugene D. Habecker's *The Other Side of Leadership.* Although each of these books makes a valuable contribution to the literature, we still struggle with the question, "What's different about Christian leadership?"

Furthermore, we still grapple with the separation between Christian leaders in the church or parachurch organization and the Christian leader who serves in a secular field. In addition to the outmoded idea that one is "ministry" and the other is "career," we also assume that the game rules for Christians in secular leadership are different. Do we really understand the ethical dilemmas of political compromise, profit margins, medical decisions, legal maneuvering, educational tradeoffs and media hype? When we address the question of Christian leadership, the principles must apply to all sectors and be meaningful to all persons whom God has called to lead.

"What's different about Christian leadership?" The most common approach to the question is found in the term "servant." Certainly, the Christlike spirit of a servant is a biblical distinction for Christian leadership. But the problem is that the concept of "servanthood" leaves us hung up on one horn of a dilemma. Jesus said, "Whoever wants to become great among you must be your servant, and whoever wants to be first, must be slave of all" (Mark 10:43 NIV). This poses a paradox. Leadership and servanthood are biblical concepts in creative tension—neither one can be exploited, neither one can be denied. To define Christian leadership as servanthood alone is to leave unanswered many of the practical problems which confront Christians in leadership roles every day. Consequently, in most circles and especially among the young, leadership and servanthood convey the image of conflicting roles. Even the hyphenated term "servant-leadership" does not keep us from swinging back and forth between these roles.

Another approach in the search for distinctive Christian leadership is to begin with the premises of secular leadership theory and raise them to a spiritual level with an overlay of biblical principles. This approach is helpful because it is backed by sound theory as well as solid theology. The weakness, however, is the starting point. By beginning with the premises of secular leadership theory, the assumptions underlying the theory are also accepted. Without a critique of those assumptions which invariably influence the motive and mission of leadership, conflicts will arise when biblical and secular assumptions clash in practice.

A sad truth is before us. If we fail to discern the motivation for leadership, our Christian principles can be overrun by secular interests. Robert Bellah, in his book *Habits of the Heart*, which may well be the best primer for defining the kind of future leaders we need, notes that radical self-interest has contaminated our model of leadership.[2] According to Bellah, "utilitarian" and "expressive" self-interest are the motivating forces behind our contemporary image of leaders whom we extol. Utilitarian self-interest is defined as "doing what we want to do for our own profit" and expressive self-interest is "being what we want to be for our own pleasure."

Translated, then, into leadership images, Bellah sees the *entrepreneur,* the *manager* and the *therapist* as the ideals of our culture. The *entrepreneur* is a person with a vision who is willing to take risks, but for self-achievement rather than the common good. Likewise, the *manager* is a model of efficiency in the control of systems and the allocation of resources, but with little regard for the moral consequences. So, both the entrepreneur and the manager need the *therapist* who makes them feel good about doing what they want to do and being what they want to be.

As far-fetched as these models of leadership based upon self-interest may seem, Christian leaders are not exempt from their influence. Recently, I received a job description for the presidency of a well-known Christian organization. Of course, the expectations included Christian beliefs, experience and compassion in a model of servanthood. But then unabashedly, qualifications for the position called for an enterprising executive who could develop new and innovative programs for the organization, a tough-minded administrator who could cut inefficient programs and a participatory leader who could raise the morale of the staff. I chuckled. Here was evidence of a Christian organization calling for a carbon copy of Bellah's leadership model. In one and the same person, they wanted an entrepreneur, a manager and a therapist. I pity the candidate whom they select. Not only will the role expectations come into conflict sooner or later, but the job description seemed to reflect an indiscriminating idealism based upon a secular model. After reading the job description, I said to myself, "God is busy." Christian leadership cannot be seduced by the subtleties of self-interest.

Introducing Incarnational Leadership

Our questions are still unanswered. In this "privileged time" when we stand together on the threshold of the twenty-first century, we need to take another look at Christian leadership from the perspective of Scripture and the example of Christ. Immediately, we confront the central fact of our faith. The Incarnation of Jesus Christ is the pivot upon which our world turns. Whether to understand His life or His leadership, we must begin with the Incarnation. Then, from the mystery of its paradox and the miracle of its resolution, the meaning of the "Word became flesh" unfolds before us. From His Incarnate character we learn the meaning of His redemptive vision, His servant strategy and His teaching task. Likewise, by experiencing the Incarnation for ourselves, we learn that Christian leaders are different in "being" as well as "doing." Our Incarnational "being" is *to embody the Spirit of Christ;* our Incarnational "doing" is *to empower His people.*

Who will lead us? What kind of leaders do we need? How are Christian leaders different? The answer is in the Incarnation.

Case in Point

In anticipation of preparing a new generation of Christian leaders for the 1990s and the twenty-first century, a national conference has been called for emerging young leaders under the age of forty. Imagine that you have been asked to keynote the conference with the assigned subject, "Profile of the Twenty-first Century Christian Leader." Within that context, you are also asked to address the issues of credibility and competence for Christian leadership in an increasingly secular age. Especially then, you are asked to define the distinction between Christian and secular leadership.

1. As an introduction to your speech, what *assumptions* about the 1990s and the twenty-first century would you make as the setting for Christian leadership?

2. What *qualifications,* natural and learned, would you include in your profile of the twenty-first century Christian leader? Can you rank them in order of importance?

3. What qualifications in your profile are common to both Christian and secular leaders?

4. Are there any differences in the qualifications of a Christian leader who serves in a secular rather than a religious profession?

5. If you were to conclude your speech by emphasizing one distinguishing quality of the twenty-first century Christian leader, what would it be?

2

Our Incarnate Model

With the punctuation of a shot heard around the world and throughout the heavens, the Gospel of John declares:

> The Word became flesh and dwelt among us, and we beheld His glory, the glory as of the only begotten of the Father, full of grace and truth.
>
> John 1:14

In this capsule sentence, the essence of Christian faith is revealed and the essentials of character for Christian leadership are implied. No verse in Scripture says more in fewer words and no verse in Scripture has caused more controversy. When John wrote these words, there was a prominent school of theologians called "Docetians" who reasoned that Jesus Christ only "appeared" to be human. John's revelation threw down the gauntlet. If his words are true, the Docetians were heretics. Later, in his own Epistle, John leaves no doubt about the truth that the Incarnation is the fulcrum upon which our faith balances. He writes:

> This is how you can recognize the Spirit of God; Every Spirit that acknowledges that Jesus Christ has come in the flesh is from God.
>
> 1 John 4:2 NIV

Centuries later, there are still those who contend that the idea of Jesus Christ being fully God and fully human is a myth perpetrated by the ambitions of His disciples and too silly for sophisticated minds. Still, our Christian faith turns on the mystery and miracle of this truth. Each time we confess our faith in the opening words of the Apostle's Creed, we reaffirm our belief in the Incarnation:

> I believe in God the Father Almighty, and in Jesus Christ, His only begotten Son, our Lord, Who was born of the Holy Spirit and the Virgin Mary . . . .

The Meaning of Incarnation

Once we confess this fact, the meaning of the Incarnation begins to open up to us. First, *Incarnation is a paradox of truth.* When "the Word became Flesh" in a divine-human encounter, all the paradoxes of eternal truth were prefigured—God and Satan, good and evil, heaven and hell, eternity and time, supernatural and natural, love and hate, sacred and profane. Before such opposites of truth—all of which are equally true—our human intelligence falters. At the same time, we have hope. Our ability to recognize and seek resolution to paradox makes us fully human and adds an intimation of immortality. Niels Bohr, the Nobel Prize winner, described his scientific search this way: "When we discover paradox, we know that we are on to something." His insight helps us with the mystery of the Incarnation. When we discover its paradox, we know that we are on to something.

Second, *Incarnation is the work of the Holy Spirit.* The divine-human paradox can never be resolved by natural means. Just as reality suggests the discontinuity between the natural and the supernatural, so the Incarnation means discontinuity between the divine and the human. Only the Holy Spirit, God's agent for the miraculous, can bridge the gap. Whether bringing worlds into being, creating man in His own image, lifting the veil of revelation, or Fathering the birth of the Divine Word in human flesh, the Holy Spirit is at work.

Third, *Incarnation is an act of creation.* A paradox cannot be resolved by choosing one truth to the exclusion of another or by compromising between truths. In either case, the paradox remains in puzzling, stressful and sometimes destructive tension. A third and higher truth is required, one that is outside the paradox and yet incorporates all the truth of both conflicting tenets. A dialectical argument between thesis and antithesis, for example, requires a creative synthesis for its resolution. Likewise, between the thesis of The Word and the antithesis of the flesh, Incarnation is the synthesis or God's creative breakthrough which resolves the paradox of truth. So, as God created something out of nothing and called it good, also through His Holy Spirit He gave birth to Jesus and called His name Emmanuel, "God with us." Wherever and whenever the Holy Spirit acts in the Incarnational paradox, we are witnesses to creation and "It is good."

The Incarnate Personality

In our text, we see a profile of the Incarnate personality of Jesus Christ. It is amazing how much we learn about Him from one verse of Scripture. It is more amazing to realize that in one sentence, we see the superlative spiritual quality of His life unfold before us:

> *His Incarnate Nature:* "The Word became Flesh."
> *His Incarnate Style:* "And lived for a while among us."
> *His Incarnate Gift:* "Full of grace and truth."
> *His Incarnate Influence:* "We have seen His glory."

To list the personal qualities of Jesus is not enough. We also need to see them as the attributes of His character which becomes the pattern for Incarnational leadership (Figure 1).

INCARNATIONAL LEADERSHIP:
THE PATTERN

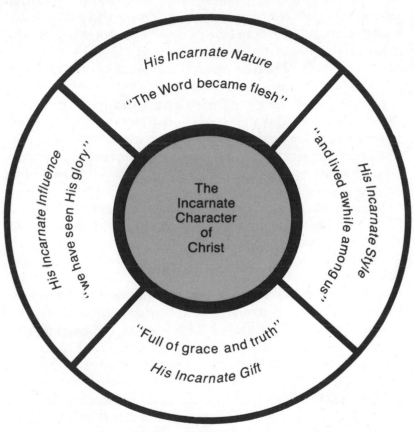

FIGURE 1

Keep in mind the fact that both the attributes of Jesus Christ and their expression in His life history are Incarnational, meaning that they are resolutions of paradox brought about by the creative action of the Holy Spirit.

Also remember that the Incarnation is not an isolated event in human history. Through the agency of the Holy Spirit, Incarnation continues in us. As Paul the apostle wrote, "For we are His workmanship, created in Jesus Christ for good

works . . ." (Ephesians 2:10). Awaiting us, then, is the experience of being born *in His likeness,* in order to live *among His
people,* serve *from His fullness* and lead *for His glory.* Initially, at
least, Incarnate Christian leaders are born, not made.

The Incarnational Process

Lest we forget, Incarnation is more than a theological con-
struct or a personality profile. It is also an interactive process
in which the character of Jesus Christ engages His environment with the strategy and the task of a leader on a mission.
The dynamic and interactive nature of this Incarnational
process is visualized in Figure 2:[1]

How are Incarnate Christian leaders different? The wheel
of the Incarnational process gives us clues and serves as the
guide for our study.

First, *the core of Incarnate Christian leadership is character*
(Part I—Our Incarnate Character: Chapter 3—"In His Likeness"). Most leadership theory begins with the behavior of the
individual within the context of the organization. Certainly,
this relationship is essential to the leadership process and cannot be neglected. But only Christian leadership begins with
the transformation of character through the work of the Holy
Spirit so that The Living Word is once again embodied in
human flesh.

Second, *the arena for Incarnate Christian leadership is culture*
(Part I—Our Incarnate Character: Chapter 4—"Among His
People"). No leader acts independently of the environment.
Incarnate leaders, in particular, are sensitive to changing
cues from the total environment—political, economic, social
and religious. In delicate balance, they identify with their culture while retaining the integrity of their character and the
objectivity of their mission.

Third, *the competence of the Incarnate Christian leader is a gift*
(Part I—Our Incarnate Character: Chapter 5—"From His
Fullness"). Always under pressure to choose between grace or
truth, the Incarnate leader seeks the heart and mind of Christ

OUR INCARNATE MODEL

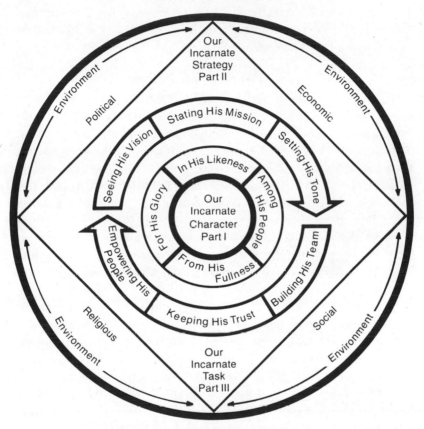

FIGURE 2

in dealing with issues, but especially in working with people. To speak the truth in love is a gift of the Holy Spirit.

Fourth, *the end of Incarnate Christian leadership is to honor God* (Part I—Our Incarnate Character: Chapter 6—"For His Glory"). All effective leaders are achievers. They are motivated and energized by high, but attainable, goals. The temptation is to take the credit and win the glory. Incarnate leaders are different. They achieve their goals, but the honor belongs to God.

Fifth, *the vision of the Incarnate Christian leader is redemptive* (Part II—Our Incarnate Strategy: Chapter 7—"Seeing His Vision"). While studies of great leaders show a concern for moral values and a commitment to human resources, Christ alone has the strategy "to seek and save the lost." Incarnate leaders see His vision as their own.

Sixth, *the mission of the Incarnate Christian leader is servanthood* (Part II—Our Incarnate Strategy: Chapter 8—"Stating His Mission"). Admittedly, every leader is a servant of sorts. Yet, as we will see, the servanthood which Christ modeled for us is distinctly different because of His singular purpose to obey the will of God and do the work of God through the sacrifice of self. An Incarnate leader is true to the same trust.

Seventh, *the tone of the Incarnate Christian leader is joy* (Part II—Our Incarnate Strategy: Chapter 9—"Setting His Tone"). Consciously or unconsciously, leaders set the tone for their organizations and their followers. The full scale can be sounded from an oppressive dirge to a lilting song. Joy, however, is the uniquely Christlike keynote of Incarnate leadership. Its quality is distinctively spiritual and its presence is fully satisfying.

Eighth, *the task of the Incarnate Christian leader is teambuilding* (Part III—Our Incarnate Task: Chapter 10—"Building His Team"). Leaders sometimes forget. Their primary resource is not time, money, space or knowledge, but people. Incarnate leaders implement their strategy through others. As seers of the vision, staters of the mission and setters of the tone, their task is teaching.

Ninth, *the test of the Incarnate Christian leader is trust* (Part III—Our Incarnate Task: Chapter 11—"Keeping His Trust"). As both the point of control and correction, the Incarnate leader is often subjected to "critical incidents" that are tests of character, strategy and task. The decisions of these times make the difference, not only between effective and ineffective leadership, but between keeping our trust and betraying our Lord.

Tenth, *the goal of the Incarnate Christian leader is to empower others* (Part III—Our Incarnate Task: Chapter 12—"Empowering His People"). All leaders have a sense of destiny. They want to be remembered as great and good. Few, however, see self-sacrifice as the means for empowering others. Christ alone gives us the Incarnate example. We are to lose ourselves for the sake of the gospel, not just to save our lives, but to extend our leadership to others who will do greater things than we have done.

Most important of all—our Incarnate model means that *every Christian is called to be a follower of Christ and a leader of others* (Epilogue: Chapter 13—"Who Will Follow Him?"). Not that the special gift of Christian leadership is equally distributed. As we approach the twenty-first century we need to pray that God will call out leaders for special tasks in the church and the world. Furthermore, the diversity and the dispersion of Christian leaders must be acknowledged and applauded. Incarnational principles, however, apply to Christian leadership in every field and wherever Christian leaders are found. So, whoever we are and whatever we do, our opportunity is to *embody* the Spirit of Christ and our responsibility is to *empower* others to do the work of Christ. After all, the story of the Gospels is how Jesus makes extraordinary leaders out of ordinary people.

Now it is time to let the Scriptures speak to us and let the example of Jesus Christ show us specifically what it means to be an Incarnate leader in character, strategy and task. His joy will be our reward.

PROLOGUE

Case in Point

In his book, *Letters to Marc about Jesus,* Henri Nouwen
describes the Incarnational process as "descending love"
and "ascending love." When Jesus emptied Himself of His
glory He began the downward move of "descending love"
which ended in total humiliation on the cross. From there,
"ascending love" took Him upward through the joy of doing
His Father's will, finishing His earthly work, and rising to
total glorification again with the Father.

Nouwen calls us to "descending love" by which we identify
with the poor, the small, the weak, the sick and the handicapped. Here, he says, we best identify with the Spirit of Jesus
Christ and participate most fully in His Incarnation. Nouwen
cites himself as the example when he left his acclaimed teaching post at Yale University for a ministry at L'ARCHE, a
community for the handicapped. Although Nouwen recom-
mends that each of us find our individual downward path of
"descending love," he still leaves most of us feeling guilty,
confused and frustrated. He himself admits that the brilliant
students at Yale may be poorer than the handicapped people
at L'ARCHE.

1. An apparent contradiction is posed between the
"descending love" of an Incarnational Christian and the
"ascending success" of a rising young Christian leader. Can
the two be reconciled?

2. In describing the "descending love" of Jesus, Nouwen
says that Christ avoided wielding influence. Yet, by definition, leadership is influence. Is this a contradiction? Or can
influence be wielded for good? If so, what is the difference
between the influence wielded by a Christian leader and a
secular leader?

3. Certainly Jesus set the example of focusing His ministry
upon the last, the least and the lost. Does this mean that He
neglected or gave up on those who were the first, had the
most and appeared whole? How can Christian leaders minister to the "up and out" as well as the "down and out"?

Part One

Our Incarnate Character

OUR INCARNATE MODEL
"IN HIS LIKENESS"

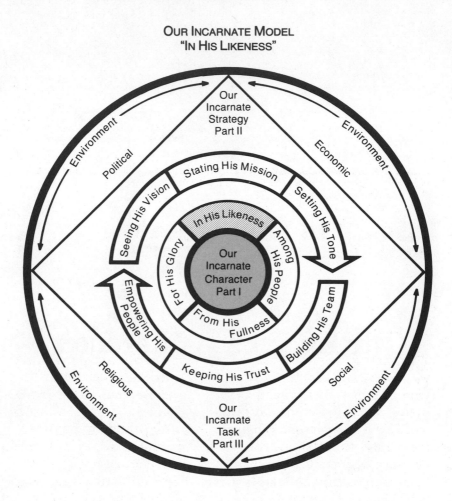

> *"The Word became flesh* and lived for awhile among us. We have seen his glory, the glory of the one and only Son, who came from the Father, full of grace and truth."
>
> John 1:14 NIV

3

In His Likeness

As the starting point for our study of Christian leadership, we asked the question, "How are Christian leaders different?" One answer comes immediately to mind. Secular leadership theory tends to emphasize the organization and the process more than the person. When secular theory does emphasize the person, the attributes of competence and charisma tend to be more important than character. A secular leader may be born with natural abilities and taught certain skills which enhance leadership quality, but the resources for leadership are limited to human dimensions. Christian leadership is different because it centers in the character of the person and engages spiritual as well as human resources. Our first paradox confronts us.

The Divine-Human Paradox

At the very heart of Christian leadership is the divine-human paradox. As we noted earlier, no phrase of Scripture

29

is more provocative than the announcement of Christ's Incarnation, "The Word became flesh. . . ." Conflicting, if not contradictory, natures come together—the eternal, holy, sovereign, transcendent and perfect nature of the Word with the sinful, fallible, earthly and mortal nature of humankind. Only faith can accept the mystery of the Incarnation and only the Spirit of God can resolve the paradox.

The Nature of the "Word"

God is a communicator. Throughout the Scriptures, He uses His "Word" to interact with His creation. God spoke the world into being, instructed patriarchs, inscribed His law, inspired His poets, commanded His prophets, affirmed His Son, left us the written Word and will judge us by the words in the Book of Life.

The meaning of "The Word" comes alive when we see its eternal and spiritual qualities identified in Scripture:

. . . the flawless Word	2 Samuel 22:31
. . . the nourishing Word	Deuteronomy 8:3
. . . the joyous Word	Jeremiah 15:16
. . . the consuming Word	Jeremiah 5:14
. . . the trustworthy Word	Psalm 93:5
. . . the truthful Word	John 17:17
. . . the eternal Word	Mark 13:31
. . . the hopeful Word	Romans 1:16
. . . the warning Word	1 Corinthians 10:11
. . . the living Word	Hebrews 4:12
. . . the probing Word	Hebrews 4:12
. . . the inspired Word	2 Timothy 3:16
. . . the enriching Word	Colossians 3:16
. . . the assuring Word	1 John 5:13
. . . the gracious Word	Luke 4:22
. . . the authoritative Word	Luke 4:32
. . . the incomparable Word	John 7:46
. . . the divine Word	John 14:24

Obviously, we can never stand before the Word of God or understand its nature. "The Divine Word" side of the Incarnational paradox leaves us impaled on the human side of our dilemma. It is too much for us.

The Nature of the "Flesh"

While the Christ of "The Word" may be too far above and beyond us, we instantly understand the meaning of the "flesh." In its Old Testament roots, the meaning of "flesh" ranged from the breadth of "all humankind" to the specificity of our "cursed" and "sinful" nature. In his Epistles, Paul persists in the negative meaning:

. . . sinful flesh   Romans 7:18
. . . enslaving flesh   Romans 7:25
. . . fatal flesh   Romans 8:8
. . . greedy flesh   Galatians 5:17
. . . destructive flesh Galatians 6:8

John, author of our Incarnational text, gives the term a similar meaning in his first Epistle when he warns against,

. . . craving flesh
. . . lustful flesh
. . . boasting flesh
1 John 2:16

Perhaps both Paul and John were influenced by Greek philosophers, beginning with Plato, who took the degraded meaning of "flesh" and assigned it to the lowest level of our human nature. Only by denying, suppressing and escaping the flesh could the idealism of the mind be attained.

John deliberately chose the term "flesh" because Greek philosophers were among his readers. His use of the term, however, does not mean that Jesus took on the nature of human sin. Rather, John means that He took its consequences into His sinless nature, suffered its wrath and died for its punishment to justify and redeem us. John also means that Jesus took on the wholeness of our humanity—body, mind, feelings and will. Nor can we forget that He took on our frailty and our flaws. Jesus was fully human. Every Christian leader can identify with the meaning of the "flesh" whether in the nature that tempts us to sin or in the flaws that keep us humble.

How did this miraculous fusion of nature come about? The difference in distance and kind between "The Word" and the "flesh" is so great that it escapes our comprehension. Writing to the Philippians, Paul gives us revealed insight into the Incarnation when he writes:

> Your attitude should be the same
> as that of Christ Jesus:
> Who, being in the very nature God,
> did not consider equality with God
> something to be grasped,
> but made himself nothing,
> taking the very nature of a servant,
> being made in human likeness.
> And being found in appearance
> as a man, he humbled himself and
> became obedient to death—
> even death on a cross!
> Philippians 2:5–8 NIV

In this Scripture, the Incarnational process is revealed: (1) the Son of God voluntarily "emptied" Himself of His own divine glory; (2) took on the nature of a servant; (3) became human through the fathering of the Holy Spirit; (4) humbled Himself and followed in obedience to the point of death; and (5) died on a criminal's cross. Away with cheap grace! At supreme cost to God, "The Word became flesh."

Enter the Holy Spirit. Only the same brooding, energizing presence which spoke the universe into being and created "man" in His own image could enact the Incarnation. To be born of the Virgin Mary, Jesus Christ had to be conceived by the Holy Spirit as His surrogate father.

It is the fusion of the divine and human that gives Jesus His integrity. Even though He took on the whole of our humanity, He lived without sin. When He challenged His enemies, "Which of you convicts me of sin?" they fell silent. Of course, His sinlessness is our hope for salvation. Upon His sinless nature, He took our sins and sacrificed His life to save us. But also, He showed us how to lead with our lives by becoming the embodiment of Christ in human form through the fathering of the Holy Spirit.

The Weakness of Secular Theory

Secular theory has little to say about the character of a leader. Although the study of leadership began many years ago with the search for the *personal traits* of good leaders, the results have been so inconclusive that some scholars have said the subject is "dead and buried." To add to the uncertainty, advanced studies of leadership show that the personal qualities effective in one situation at a given point in time may not be successful in another situation at another point in time. Consequently, students of leadership have retreated into generalities which most of us believe but cannot support with conclusive evidence. Sharplin, for instance, suggests that a good leader is human, farsighted, inspired and confident.[1] Character is inferred in support of these qualities, but not specified in either content or quality.

Studies of *leadership style* also infer the character of the person. James MacGregor Burns draws the distinction between transformational and transactional leadership styles.[2] A transformational leader is one who inspires others to follow by the sheer force of a personality that is creative, eloquent, energetic and attractive. Jesus would qualify as a transformational leader when He called Peter, James and John from their fishing business with the invitation, "Come, follow Me and I will make you to become fishers of men."

A transactional leader is almost the opposite, but may be just as effective. As the term "transactional" implies, the process of leadership is more important than the person. By interacting with the people who are identified as followers, the transactional leader fashions a vision for the future out of their collective needs and dreams. The image of the military general during the French Revolution comes to mind. As the mob surged through the streets toward the Bastille, he stepped out on his balcony, surveyed the scene and ordered his aide, "Quick. My tunic and my sword. I am their leader and I must follow them."

Still, studies of personality traits and leadership styles miss the heart of the matter. Presumably, even scoundrels can be good leaders. Perhaps not in the future, however. The all-seeing eye of the media is putting the character of leaders under microscopic scrutiny. The scandals of Ivan Boesky in finance, Michael Deaver in government, and the "Jimmys"— Bakker and Swaggart—in religion will influence attitudes toward leadership for years to come. Despite some concern about media invasion into the privacy of these persons, the scrutiny will continue and public expectations will be brutal. Secular or Christian leaders must be prepared for the most minute character checks, not only from the media, but from their constituencies as well.

Incarnation Continues

Our Incarnational model makes the character of the person the essential ingredient for Christian leadership. We may sag at the thought because none of us qualifies as perfect in character. Rather, we feel like the brutally honest political campaign manager who confessed after the Gary Hart scandal, "None of us can afford to be frisked." At best we can say with Carlyle as he turned away from the sneering mob at the hanging of a criminal, "There, but for the grace of God, go I."

The divine-human tension is in all of us. We aspire to godliness, but lapse into our humanness. Paul voiced our frustration in Romans when he wrote:

When I want to do good, evil is right there with me. For in my inner being I delight in God's law; but I see another law at work in the members of my body, waging war against the law of my mind and making me a prisoner of the law of sin at work within my members. What a wretched man I am! Who will rescue me from this body of death?

Romans 7:21–24 NIV

Incarnational leadership seems to be beyond our grasp. But we can take heart. In the Incarnational process by which the "Word became flesh" in the person of Jesus Christ, we see our hope. The same Spirit of God who brought to life the divine Word in human flesh is able to bring to birth the likeness of Christ in our humanity.

Paul sees the outcome of this miraculous action in his favorite phrase, "Christ in us." He repeats the phrase many times in his writings and usually adds a personal quality of life that gives us the profile of a person in whom the Incarnation continues:

. . . new life in Christ Jesus	Romans 6:23
. . . unity in Christ Jesus	Romans 12:5
. . . sanctification in Christ Jesus	1 Corinthians 1:2
. . . freedom in Christ Jesus	Galatians 2:4
. . . faith in Christ Jesus	Galatians 2:16
. . . blessing in Christ Jesus	Ephesians 1:3
. . . created in Christ Jesus	Ephesians 2:10
. . . forgiven in Christ Jesus	Ephesians 4:32
. . . hope in Christ Jesus	Colossians 1:27
. . . perfect in Christ Jesus	Colossians 1:28
. . . reality in Christ Jesus	Colossians 2:17
. . . grace in Christ Jesus	1 Timothy 2:1
. . . salvation in Christ Jesus	1 Timothy 2:1

To repeat, Incarnation is not an isolated event in human history. It is a continuing act of creation by which we can gain the integrity of character which qualifies us for Incarnational leadership.

Our integrity, however, is not our own. Isaiah, with his pin-point prophetic accuracy, views all our attempts at righteousness as "filthy rags." Only through the fathering of the Holy Spirit can we know the reality of "Christ in us." Think what this means. As Christ lived out the Word of God through human flesh, so we can express the Spirit of Christ through our humanity.

Incarnation continues—in human bodies which are temples where the Spirit of Christ dwells, in human intellect renewed by the mind of Christ and in human wills totally obedient to the will of God. With "Christ in us" we live as He lived, think as He thought, give as He gave, hurt as He hurt, weep as He wept, serve as He served and lead as He led.

The Gift of Incarnation

Incarnation for Jesus Christ started with His divine nature as the "Word" of God. For us, the starting point is the grim reality of our sin-flawed and death-bound flesh. This means that we must start where Jesus Christ finished, being obedient to the point of death, even the death of the cross! Around this truth there is neither ambiguity nor paradox. With the precision of the surgeon's scalpel, Jesus Christ commands us, "Take up your cross and follow Me." Whereas the Incarnation for Christ began with His "emptying," our Incarnation begins with our "dying." This is a voluntary act, but absolutely essential to the miracle in which our flesh becomes the Word of "Christ in us." No biblical truth is more clear:

> For we who are alive are always being given over to death for Jesus' sake, so that his life may be revealed in our mortal body.
>
> 2 Corinthians 4:11 NIV

By this act of obedience unto death, we are resurrected in the newness of life and in the likeness of Jesus Christ. In other words, "Christ in us" is born through the fathering of the Holy Spirit just as He, the Divine Word, was born of the Virgin Mary, in human flesh.

Once Christ is born in us, Incarnation continues as we take on the very nature of a servant and empty ourselves of self-glory. Then and only then are we ready to be appointed and anointed as Incarnate leaders in the Spirit and for the sake of Jesus Christ. We see the Incarnational process revealed in Christ and reversed for us in Figure 3 on page 38.

The Discipline of Incarnation

Of course, the Incarnation of Jesus Christ in us is a gift of grace. Neither our merit nor our works can earn us His presence. Incarnation comes only when we are crucified and resurrected with Him. Yet, Incarnation is a developing relationship as well as an experiential gift to be received. Each day we die; each day we are reborn in the Spirit of Christ; each day we take the form of a servant; and each day we empty ourselves of our own glory.

Self-preservation, self-esteem and self-worth are strong and legitimate drives for leaders. As in the case of Jesus, the extension of these drives into self-love, self-conceit and self-glory can also be the most insidious temptations for those who lead. Each day brings decisions that require risks, test motives and reflect character. Only the daily discipline of dying with Christ and being resurrected in His likeness will prepare us for these decisions and deliver us from their temptations. As a person who has been in leadership positions for almost forty years, I treat the addiction to power like an addiction to alcohol. Each morning I pray,

> Lord, as I begin this day, let me take up my cross and die with You. Then, through the power of your Holy Spirit, may I be raised in Your likeness so that I may serve in Your Spirit, risking my life for others and not caring who gets the credit.
> Amen

Otherwise, power can be intoxicating. Incarnational leaders are born of the Spirit and made by self-discipline.

THE INCARNATIONAL PROCESS

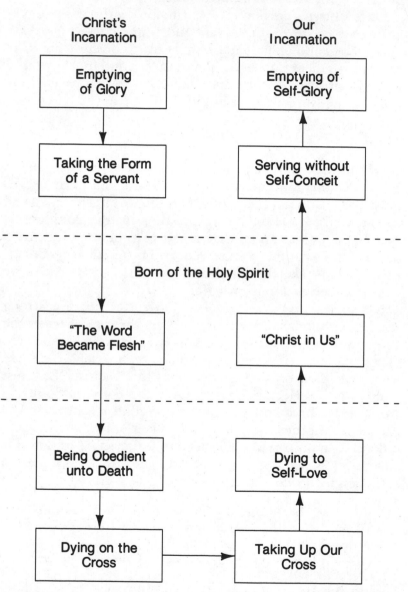

Figure 3

Case in Point

Burnout is an occupational hazard for leaders. Business has a reputation for expending leadership resources on a relatively short cycle and then providing the financial benefits of a "golden parachute" for early retirement. Religious organizations are not so generous. Leaders are expected to serve for a lifetime and to retire on minimum compensation.

The burnout cycle for leaders, whether secular or Christian, is similar. In the *first stage* of a career, high enthusiasm, total commitment and high energy characterize their leadership. After a period of time, however, enthusiasm gives way to stagnation, the *second stage*. The role becomes boring, the work routine and vision blurred. When this happens, a *third stage* is entered. Depending upon the personality, the leader gets angry, withdraws or escapes into the self-destructive patterns of alcohol, drugs, divorce, or emotional illness. At this stage, unless the person is helped by some form of therapeutic intervention, he or she will become a full-fledged victim of *four-stage* burnout, apathetic and beyond caring.

1. To our surprise, Christian leaders are at higher risk for burnout than their secular colleagues. Some suggest that their idealism becomes disillusionment because the expectations are too high, the criticism is too great and the results are too intangible. Do you agree? Does the pattern fit Christian leaders whom you know who have become victims of burnout?

2. The burnout cycle is highly individualized. What are the signals that you see in yourself when you are in danger of entering the burnout cycle? What do you do for renewal?

3. Is the Incarnational experience of "Christ in you" a preventative for burnout? Why? What resources are made available in the Incarnational experience for Christian leaders whether in secular or religious careers?

OUR INCARNATE MODEL
"AMONG HIS PEOPLE"

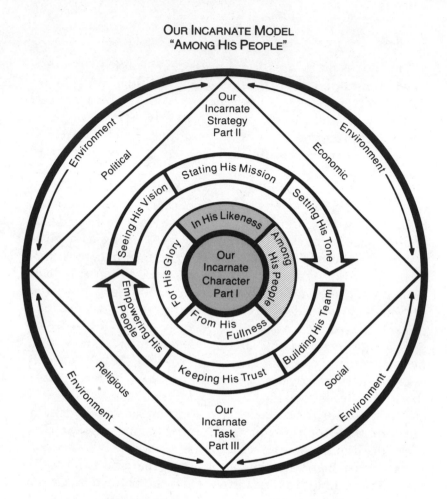

> The Word became flesh *and lived for a while among us.* We have seen his glory, the glory of the one and only Son, who came from the Father, full of grace and truth.
>
> John 1:14 NIV

4

Among His People

Jesus Christ, the Incarnate person, did not remain isolated from the culture into which He was born. His Incarnate character as well as His strategy and His task were profoundly influenced by the culture and time in which He lived.

Our text progresses from the nature of Christ identified as "The Word became flesh" to the culture in which He led and served. We read, "the Word became flesh" and "lived for a while among us." John utilizes a memorable Old Testament image to help us understand what he means. The more literal translation comes from that image, "He pitched His tent among us" or "He tabernacled among us."

In our mind's eye, we see the nomadic horde of Israelites wandering in the wilderness of Sinai. During the day they marched and at night they pitched their tents. From a bird's eye view, they might have looked like an army of aimless ants. But a closer look would show at the center of their company a rough-hewn box inlaid with gold that housed the Presence of God. Either image, a tent or a tabernacle, is Incarnational.

41

The pitching of the tent suggests Jesus' identification with the nomadic nature and marginal existence of the people of Israel. Tabernacling, however, suggests His sacred Presence in the midst of their spiritual wandering—the ever-present symbol of hope that God would make good His promise and lead them to a homeland. Another paradox is before us.

The Sacred-Secular Paradox

In the Incarnational character of Jesus Christ, His divine and human natures were poised in a tension that could only be synthesized by the creative Spirit of God. Now the time perspective of Jesus Christ is in tension with His culture. His perspective is sacred and eternal; the culture is secular and temporal. At best, interaction between the two is a risk. How does an Incarnational leader interact with the culture? Is the sacred maintained in isolation? Immersed in complete identification? Compartmentalized into sacred and secular parts? Or critically involved with a view to change?

Incarnational leadership is neither isolated, immersed or compartmentalized within the culture. When Jesus pitched His tent among us it meant that He not only took on the whole of our humanity as a person but also identified with us in our cultural character. Yet He maintained the objectivity of His spiritual viewpoint. From that perspective, He could understand His culture, assess its values and its needs, identify with its people and respond to its demands.

For years, leadership theory ignored the culture within which leaders were expected to serve. Of course, effective leaders were sensitive to the needs of their followers, but by and large, the particular values, norms and customs that gave personality to a cultural or organizational setting were ignored. Instead, it was assumed that a leader could be effective in any setting at any time. Then, as the influence of the culture became recognized, the "contingency theory" of leadership developed.[1] Simply put, the effectiveness of the leader became contingent upon the setting, timing and circumstances. No longer was it assumed that effective leadership could automatically transfer from one organization to another or from one time to another in the same organization. The nature of the setting and the timing of the circumstances could either enhance or deter effective leadership. In his book *Talking Straight,* Lee Iacocca draws upon this wisdom when he cites the reasons why he refused to be a candidate for the presidency of the United States.[2] Iacocca said that he was too old to start another career. He knows that politics and the presidency represent a change of worlds for an automobile executive. Successful leadership in one field does not automatically transfer to another career.

Conversely, a Christian executive in higher education gained national stature for his wisdom in handling protesters at a state university in the tumultuous days of the late 1960s and early 1970s. Later, he accepted the presidency of a comparatively small Christian liberal arts college. When I visited him in the early days of his administration, he spoke about his goals of winning substantial funding from national foundations, building a scholarly reputation for the faculty and attracting the best and the brightest of Christian students.

As I listened to him speak, I realized that he had superimposed his own expectations upon his new institution without adequate regard for the culture of this particular Christian college. I left shaking my head and predicting that he would soon be shocked by a change of educational cultures that might better be described as a change of worlds. Eighteen months later this outstanding executive and spiritual leader resigned his post. He had the credentials but he misread the culture.

Leadership literature has now taken another step toward understanding the culture of organizations and its relationship to effective leadership. Rational analysis of an organization based upon numbers or described by charts is not enough. The intangible qualities and informal flow of an organization as revealed through its culture may be more important to understanding how and why leaders succeed or fail. In most instances, these intangibles are perceived by intuition rather than statistical data. Of course, a culture includes formalized information that can be studied, but it also includes the less formal customs, rituals, celebrations, heroes and stories.

A pastor accepted the invitation to serve a large metropolitan church which was well-known for its Scandinavian origins. In the land of "Johnsons," "Swansons" and "Andersons" the pastor's Welsh name instantly put upon him a severe handicap. Also, even though the church had discontinued an alternate worship in the mother tongue two years before his arrival, the pastor knew neither the taste nor the meaning of "lutefisk."

Clerical colleagues in the community gave him little chance of survival. Neither did I until I visited him. After a meeting in his study where we talked frankly about the ethnic barriers that had to be surmounted before he could get to the gospel, he mentioned one of his earliest encounters with the culture. When the recreation center had to be repainted, the committee insisted on the strong and bold colors of blue and yellow. At first the pastor started to object, but then he remembered, "Those are the colors of the Swedish flag." With sensitivity of spirit, he said nothing and then concurred with the decision. When I heard him tell the story I felt sure that he would survive to serve. He has.

No doubt, Jesus Christ was a student of His culture as well as a student of His people. We misread the verse, "He knew what was in man." Perhaps in self-defense, we want to interpret this Scripture as proof of Jesus' omniscience—an attribute of His divinity. But if so, it puts insight into human nature out of our reach. Without denying His deity one iota, I prefer to interpret the phrase as evidence that Jesus had a Spirit-sharpened sensitivity to human nature. This puts an Incarnate gift within our reach. Through attention, experience, compassion, study and prayer we too can know what is "in" men and women—at least enough to understand their motives, gain their trust, serve their needs and share their dreams.

My career has taken our family from Michigan to Washington State and back to Kentucky, or from the regions of the Midwest to the Northwest and back to the South. Until you have made the moves, you may not know that they involve a change of worlds. Growing up in Michigan, I remember the formal pride that we had in our state song, "Michigan, My Michigan." We learned it in school but seldom sang it. Later, when we moved to Washington State, a culture which still has the rugged individualism of the pioneer, I never heard the state song, although I presume that there is one.

Coming back to Kentucky we encountered a weight of tradition which we never knew in Michigan or Washington. At the first University of Kentucky football game that we attended, the former governor of the state opened the season and the ceremonies by singing "My Old Kentucky Home." When his voice cracked with emotion on the phrase, "Weep no more my lady," I looked around the stadium to see the men and women of Kentucky dabbing at their eyes as they sang along.

Later, I found out that I could not win a southern audience by telling those marvelous Kentucky mountain stories in a fake southern drawl. One gracious but dead-serious woman met me after a speech in Atlanta, Georgia, to say, "I appreciated everything you had to say except your joke. It isn't funny in the South." Anyone who leads must understand the culture, its idiosyncrasies and the sensitivities of its people.

Scanning our Culture

Jesus knew His culture and people so well that He could make an accurate assessment of its readiness for His leadership and its potential for change. In one way or another, He asked the critical questions which penetrate to the heart of a culture:

What does the culture reward? Punish?
Who are the heroes of the culture? Villains?
What are the myths and tales of the culture?
At what does the culture laugh? And cry?

What does the culture celebrate? Mourn?
What are its taboos?
Is it a young, middle-aged or old culture?

For just a moment, look at the culture in which Jesus chose
to live in the light of these questions:

It rewarded wealth and power;
It punished nonconformity;
Its heroes were Old Testament prophets;
Its villains were the Romans;
Its stories were epics of Jewish heroes dying for freedom;
It celebrated religious festivals;
It mourned death and sickness, long and loud;
Its taboos were sexual;
It was an old culture with a glorious past and an uncertain
   hope for political and spiritual freedom with the coming
   of the Messiah.

Or, more specifically, look at Jesus' culture this way. Our
Incarnational model shows four environmental facets within
which the leader must work:

- *Political power* resided in Roman hands with the symbol
  of the Roman eagle over doorways, the image of Caesar
  on coins, legions bullying their way through the streets
  and Roman law ruling in the courts.
- *Economic power* weighed heavily in the hands of a few,
  most of whom gained their wealth through cheating, corruption and collusion which left the masses in ghettoes of
  poverty with no escape.
- *Social power* divided itself horizontally among the
  Romans, Jewish leaders, nobility and merchants and
  vertically in a caste system of ethnic origin, religious
  orthodoxy, economic standing and educational achievement with no hope for upward mobility.
- *Religious power* fit compactly into an airtight system of
  doctrine and practice which the Pharisees regulated, the
  Scribes interpreted, and the Sadducees debated so that a

vital faith was unnecessary and spiritual freedom was impossible.

Thorough search of the Gospels shows that Jesus remained sensitive to all the norms and customs of His culture which did not violate human dignity, restrict the gospel or oppress the poor. When we come to study His strategy, we will see that He turned the political, economic, social and spiritual threats of His culture into opportunities to preach the gospel.

The Incarnate Risk

Incarnational leadership is a risk. By "pitching His tent among us" Jesus became vulnerable to criticism. When He made His choice with the poor, He risked the wrath of the rich. When He made His choice with sinners, He evoked the wrath of the righteous. When He turned from political power, He lost the freedom fighters. Yet, because He excelled as a student of His culture, every decision was deliberate. He knew the history of the Hebrews so well that He could not be trapped by trick questions. He knew the conflict between the Jews and the Romans so well that He could not get caught in the middle of their fight.

Tension between the sacred and the secular always exists for a leader. To what extent do we identify with our people? To what extent do we remain objective? Most of us who were schooled in administration or management in the '50s, '60s and '70s were drilled in the principles formulated by Peter Drucker as "Management by Objective." I can still see the pyramidal charts with the layers for the objective, goals, strategies and tactics. "MBO" or Management By Objective is certainly worthwhile, but it is like a skeleton without flesh and blood. "MBO" must be complemented by "MBWA" or Management By Walking Around.

When you read Jack Eckerd's book entitled *Eckerd: Finding the Right Prescription,* you find the secret of his success in his practice of stopping at Eckerd Drugstores and visiting personally with his employees.[3] Sure, Jack risks his executive image when he stocks shelves with his employees, but he gains a far greater value. His people know, as Jack himself says, that the "Old Man" cares. Slowly, but surely, we are learning that the most effective leaders are not wasting their time when they listen to the stories, participate in the rituals of their organization, work alongside their followers and celebrate the heroes of their culture. To be effective, a leader must understand and build a strong culture.

Identifying with His People

Of course, the culture is no more than the composite of the history and hopes, values and traditions of its people. When Jesus pitched His tent among us, it means that He not only took on the whole of our humanity, but He also took the risk of identifying with us. We sometimes forget the significance of the thirty silent years between His birth and public ministry. During that time He grew as a member of a large family, the son of a carpenter, in a small town in Nazareth. Literally, He became nothing and took on the very nature of a servant. His identification with His culture was so complete that His own townsfolk ridiculed His teaching and rejected His miracles. Yet, we read that the common folk heard Him gladly, religious leaders admitted that He taught with authority and civil authorities could find no fault in Him. By living among us, Jesus gained the commitment of His followers, the confidence of the public and the begrudging respect of religious and political leaders.

As another example of cultural sensitivity, our oldest son is a management consultant. Among his clients are two corporations—one a world leader in aircraft production. High technology is its livelihood and yet, because it started out as a small family firm, he is called in to survey the attitudes of thousands of employees, compile the results, set up discussion groups on critical issues and make recommendations to the management because they want to remain sensitive to human needs.

In contrast, another company which has skyrocketed

overnight to world identity in the field of high technology calls him in to "trouble shoot" when the organizational system breaks down and people are at each other's throats. At times, it appears as if people are only extensions of the computer circuits they design. The board meetings are said to be shouting matches, big money is the reward system and heads roll at a moment's notice. When asked to consider a top management position in the firm, my son answered, "No, I'm a people person. I could never survive." Keep in mind the fact that both companies, with contrasting cultures, are immensely successful.

Our conclusion is that the Incarnational Christian leader must be a discerning student as well as a loving servant of the culture in which he or she is called to lead. Is this not what Jesus meant when He sent His disciples into the world with this petition to His Father?

> As You have sent Me into the world, I also have sent them into the world. And for their sakes I sanctify Myself, that they also may be sanctified by the Truth.
>
> John 17:18–19

We who are willing to take the risk of living among our people can count on Jesus Christ continuing to pray this prayer for us and on the Holy Spirit responding with Incarnate grace to keep us sanctified for His purpose at the same time that we identify with His people. Until we "pitch our tent" among our people and become one of them without compromising the spirit of "Christ in Us," no one will follow us.

Case in Point

A corporate executive inherited the family firm and fortune. Soon, he found that he hated to get up in the morning and seriously considered a change of careers into a more "Christian" profession. While in turmoil, he prayed and God showed him what he had been missing. His employees suffered all the symptoms of personal and professional trauma which were common to any secular industry. Then and there, he saw his ministry—to create a more humane working environment and offer support services for the personal needs of his employees.

A new world opened up to him. In addition to taking leadership in profit-sharing, communication and participation programs within the company, he also responded to the wide range of his employees' needs. Before a person was fired for poor performance, alcoholism or absenteeism, for instance, counseling became an option. Bible study groups, sometimes with nationally known speakers, met weekly on a volunteer basis.

To emphasize the importance of families, a recreational center was purchased and programs were designed around family activities. Even the cultural, educational and spiritual climate of the community was included in his extended ministry. Through family and company contributions, the small city became a model for historical renovation, imaginative expansion, social services and community spirit.

Years later, the Christian executive is fully alive each day, finding new ways to serve his employees, fathering his extended family and being fiercely dedicated to a Sunday school class of high school students who include both children of wealth and wards of the court. Most amazing of all, a visitor to his office (though he may be head of a multimillion dollar business) may have to wait while the executive counsels a troubled teenager. According to his secretary, they have priority.

1. When the corporate executive began to "live" among

his people, his outlook changed and he found new meaning in life. Think about the people whom you are called to lead and serve. What are their needs? How can you identify with your people and still enhance your leadership role?

2. What is the culture of your organization? Its key values? Behavioral norms? Prevailing customs? Special rituals? Historical myths?

3. What changes in your leadership style and agenda might you make to be more responsive to the needs of your people?

OUR INCARNATE MODEL
"FROM HIS FULLNESS"

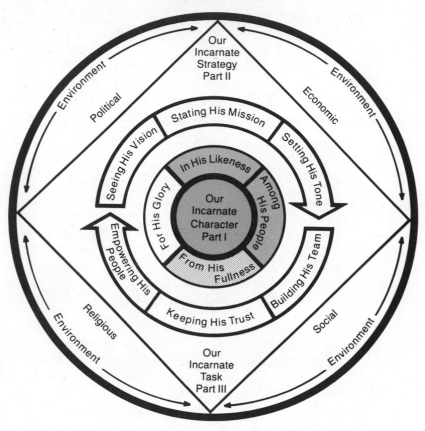

The Word became flesh and made his dwelling among us. We have seen his glory, the glory of the one and only, who came from the Father, *full of grace and truth.*

John 1:14 NIV

5

From His Fullness

Personal traits are fundamental to the quality of leadership. For years, researchers have tried to find the distinguishing personality traits of effective leaders. Sort through the studies and a long list results. An effective leader is above average in such traits as: sociability, initiative, persistence, getting things done, self-confidence, insight, cooperation, popularity, adaptability and verbal skills. Certainly, these traits are important, although the research also finds that every situation is different. The traits for successful leadership in one situation may not bring success in another setting.

Incarnational leadership depends upon certain fundamental traits. They apply to spiritual leadership in any situation. They are so foundational that all other traits are complementary. Those traits are revealed in our text when we read that The Word which became flesh and dwelt among us was "full of grace and truth." When John Gardner, the perceptive author of such books as *Excellence* and *Self-Renewal,* proposed a list of traits that are indispensable to excellence in leadership, he wrote, "Look for taste and judgment, everything else is a dime a dozen." We may say the same. When we search for Incarnational leaders, look for persons who are "full of grace and truth." Everything else is "a dime a dozen."

The Grace—Truth Paradox

Here again are two dimensions of the Incarnational character of Jesus Christ which are in paradoxical tension. In simplest terms, "grace" is God *giving* Himself to us and "truth" is God *revealing* Himself to us. Although they are not contradictory, they are opposite expressions of His character, equally true and sometimes in apparent conflict.

The Meaning of Grace

We remember Jesus as a person "full of grace." Not by accident, John puts grace before truth when He identifies the Incarnational traits of Jesus. We cannot stand before His truth, but we are saved by His grace. The Scriptures show us its meaning:

. . . grace is free	Psalm 84:11
. . . grace is self-sacrificing	2 Corinthians 8:9
. . . grace is sufficient	2 Corinthians 12:9
. . . grace is rich	Ephesians 1:7
. . . grace is glorious	Philippians 4:19

We may forget that Jesus lived by the gift of grace. Not only did He pray, "Give us our daily bread" as evidence of His dependence upon the grace of God, but He always gave thanks for the bread He received. Gratitude to God and giving to others are complementary expressions of the fullness of grace in Incarnational leadership. "Thank you" and "Can I help?" are naturally and regularly heard from the lips of leaders who have received the gift of grace.

For us, the "fullness of grace" in Jesus Christ has special meaning. In gratitude for the grace of God in His life, Jesus sacrificed Himself for our salvation. Monumental truth rises before us when we read:

> There is no difference, for all have sinned and fall short of the glory of God, and are justified freely by his grace through the redemption that came by Christ Jesus.
> Romans 3:22–24 NIV

The whole plan of redemption comes into focus in the words, ". . . justified freely by his grace." Self-sacrifice is the ultimate expression of gratitude for the grace of God.

The Meaning of Truth

"Truth" as well as "grace" were fully incarnate in Jesus Christ. He not only showed how God gives Himself to us in grace, but also how He reveals Himself through truth. The contrast between truth and grace is hard to handle. In the Scriptures, truth confronts us as an absolute standard:

. . . truth is perfect	Deuteronomy 32:4
. . . truth is sovereign	2 Samuel 7:28
. . . truth is impartial	Zechariah 8:16
. . . truth is sworn	Isaiah 65:16
. . . truth is to be obeyed	Galatians 5:7
. . . truth exposes falsehood	Proverbs 12:22
. . . truth may be rejected	Romans 2:8
. . . truth may be celebrated	1 Corinthians 13:6
. . . truth is to be believed	2 Thessalonians 2:13

The contrast between grace and truth is clear. Grace is a free gift, truth is an absolute command. Grace may be received, truth must be obeyed. Grace cannot be earned, truth can be learned. Whereas grace is a gift, truth is a standard; whereas grace is an option, truth is a requirement.

John's Gospel illustrates the meaning of truth. Twenty-eight times in the Gospel, Jesus says, "I tell you the truth . . . ." Each time He reveals something about the character of God or His Word it drops like an eternal plumbline into the midst of His hearers. From then on, all human behavior is measured against that plumbline. On one side is freedom; on the other is bondage. The truth may be believed or denied, accepted or distorted, obeyed or rejected, hated or celebrated—but it remains as the measure against which all will be judged.

The "Fullness" of Grace and Truth

When John writes that Jesus Christ expressed the "fullness" of grace and truth, he reveals another Incarnational resource for us. In this case, "fullness" does not mean "perfection" in the divine sense, but "wholeness" in the divine-human or Incarnational sense. Grace and truth so pervaded His person in coactive relationship that everything He said and did expressed these motives. If you asked anyone who met Jesus to describe His dominant traits in a word or two, the answer would come back, "Grace and truth."

Again, we are in the realm where the Holy Spirit works. The same "fullness" of grace and truth is available to us when we are reborn with "Christ in us." "Fullness of grace" is ours just as Paul sent Titus to complete the act of grace in the lives of the Christians at Corinth:

> But just as you excel in everything—in faith, in speech, in knowledge, in complete earnestness and in your love for us—see that you also excel in this grace of giving.
>
> 2 Corinthians 8:7 NIV

Equally so, we have the promise of the "fullness of truth" in the inspired words of Paul to the believers at Colossae:

> I have become its servant by the commission God gave me to present to you the Word of God in its fullness—the mystery that has been kept hidden for ages and generations, but is now disclosed to the saints.
>
> Colossians 1:25–26 NIV

Our gifts of grace may not be perfect and our grasp of truth may not be omniscient, but they can be so full in us that they characterize our being. All we do and say will demonstrate the synergism of the Holy Spirit when we are ". . . speaking the truth in love" (Ephesians 4:15).

Dr. James Gregory served as the President of Spring Arbor College in Michigan when I attended there. His spirit breathed the beauty of Christ and his mind had an uncanny edge of biblical truth. None of us students could ever imagine a harsh word or a tough decision coming from him. But from him I learned about ". . . speaking the truth in love."

At Homecoming time, dormitories held an open house for parents and visitors. Prizes were given for the best-decorated rooms. My roommate and I decided to make fun of this "kid stuff" by shocking the visitors who ignored the "no trespassing" sign on our door. We built a "one-holer" outhouse in the middle of our room complete with a path and Sears catalog. Needless to say, our guests were shocked when they opened the door. They reported us to the Dean of Men who closed down our project. On Monday following Homecoming, President Gregory called me into his office. I had become one of his prize students in philosophy and he had become my mentor.

Gentle as always, President Gregory invited me to a chair and then, eye-to-eye, began to speak, "David, Western civilization has certain proprieties and Christian colleges have certain expectations about taste and judgment. You violated them both by your display at Homecoming. I trust that it will not happen again. If it does, I shall be forced to take decisive action."

Without raising his voice or invoking punishment, he crushed me. No lesson of my freshman year was so powerful or so lasting. I learned that a Christian leader can be tough-minded and tender-hearted, ". . . speaking the truth in love" and demonstrating the "fullness" of grace and truth.

The Wisdom of the Spirit

How and when do we show grace or speak the truth? Following the example of Jesus Christ, Incarnational leaders need the discerning gift of the Spirit to know when to act with grace and when to speak the truth with love.

First, it is important to note that *grace precedes truth.* Christian leaders can succumb to the temptation to speak the truth without love, especially in positions of power.

Second, we must remember that *there is a time for grace and a time for truth.* Only as the Holy Spirit gives us the mind of Christ can we discern the difference.

Third, *we must avoid contaminating both grace and truth by trying to cushion the truth between layers of grace.* A "grace-truth-grace" sandwich cannot be digested by those to whom we feed it.

We fail in our leadership when we establish our style on either extreme of grace or truth. Early in my career, I developed the reputation of a bright visionary, an incisive thinker and a hard-nosed administrator who spoke the truth without a glint of grace in the eye. Because images of leadership tend to persist, I have spent the rest of my career backfilling my leadership with the gift of grace. To compensate for the speed and crispness with which I tend to speak the truth, I have often erred on the side of grace—avoiding confrontation under the rationalization that I was saving people and letting issues slide when the evidence predicted disaster. Or I have put together "grace-truth-grace" sandwiches in which I tried to make strong truth more palatable by slices of soggy grace. Almost without exception, when I have tried to show grace against the evidence of truth or speak the truth without grace, I have lived to regret my decision.

Incarnational leaders know when to show grace and when to speak the truth in love. In general, we can follow the principle practiced by Jesus: *show grace to people; speak the truth to issues; and don't confuse the two.* We will not go far wrong if we follow this principle. But there is a maturity implied in the "fullness" of grace and truth which permits us an exception. At times, the plumbline of truth is more gracious than grace itself. Too many times, I have tried to be redemptive by being gracious. Rather than resolving the problem, however, I have muddied the issue, prolonged the problem and lost the person. As delicate as the surgeon's scalpel, there is a time for the "redemptive incision"—putting painful truth on the line, drawing strict guidelines for changing behavior or letting the person go. Many times we mistake our cowardice or sloppiness for grace. One of the most severe indictments of a Christian college that I know is to hear students say, "It is easier to ask forgiveness than it is to get permission." Neither grace nor truth is honored in such a system.

Grace for Grace

But if we err, we must err on the side of grace. More often than not, it will cost us something—a slice of power, a glitter of reputation, an edge of criticism, a pain in the pit of the stomach, a loss of sleep and even the lesson of failure. Yet, if we act with the "fullness" of grace which puts people first and the fullness of truth which gives us the assurance of being fair and doing right, we will have peace. Even now, I look back upon a decision in which I waffled on incisive, truth-supported action because I lacked the heart for confrontation. Every time I turned around, the issue surfaced again to absorb my time and drain my energy. If I could go back, I would make the incisive redemptive cut. My cowardice shames me, and yet, the desire to redeem the person and save a situation played some part in my decision. History will have to be the judge. Somehow I sense that, even through my muddling, grace will prevail.

John confirms the "fullness of grace and truth" when he follows our Incarnational text with the testimony:

> From the fullness of his grace we have all received one blessing after another. For the law was given through Moses; grace and truth came through Jesus Christ.
> John 1:16–17 NIV

The New King James version is even more graphic in its translation, "From his fullness we have all received, grace for grace." Two images are contained in the passage. "Grace for grace" may be likened to the waves of the sea, one following another without ceasing. The "fullness of his grace" does mean endless blessings, one after another.

In the same image of the ocean waves, another meaning is hidden. Action and reaction make up the movement of the waves that crash on the shore. A whitecap coming in meets another going out. Not unlike the paradox that pits one truth against another in the Incarnation, "grace for grace" assures us of the presence and guidance of God's Spirit in the unexplainable conflicts and apparent contradictions which dog the footsteps of our human existence. Conflicts and contradictions, as well as mysteries and miracles, serve as the raw material with which Incarnate leaders must work. The assurance of "grace for grace" is the source of our confidence, the antidote to stress, and the court of last resort when we must make decisions without all the facts or without a guarantee on the consequences.

In sum, the fullness of grace and truth is another outcome of "Christ in us." Through the coming of His Holy Spirit and by His continuing counsel, we will receive and cultivate these gifts as the traits for which our leadership is remembered. The danger is developing a leadership style around only one side of the paradox—either soft-hearted grace or hard-nosed truth. Equally imbalanced is an attempt to sandwich the strong meat of truth between the slices of grace when we deal with people. If we have the discerning mind of Christ we will know when to show grace and when to speak the truth in love. When in doubt, grace must lead and prevail, even at personal sacrifice. After all, Incarnational leadership means showing grace to others in gratitude for the grace we have received and speaking the truth in love without counting our personal cost.

Case in Point

A promising Christian leader in his twenties with a lively interest in politics took a staff position in an association which was led by a president who was also a highly respected and successful lobbyist. Under his tutelage over a period of time, the young man's energy and brilliance won him the position as vice president.

Soon after he began working closely with the president, he noted a marked change in his behavior. The president's pattern of coming late to work, spending long hours alone in his office and often missing appointments and deadlines came to light. By accident, the vice president discovered that the president was an alcoholic with aggravated physical problems.

Before long the reputation and work of the association began to suffer. During a critical legislative session, the young man met an ethical conflict which forced him to choose between truth and grace. He tried to minister to his mentor by sobering him up in the office and getting him home safely at night. He also doubled his own work load by appearing for the president at legislative appointments and hearings. When he did, the president in his sober moments accused him of trying to get his job. This added to the vice president's dilemma because he also felt a moral obligation to inform the Board of Directors about the problem, but to do so would mean going around his boss and risking retaliation. He calls you for advice.

1. What is his first responsibility—to his president, to the critical legislative program, or to the Board of Directors?

2. Should he continue to help his mentor out of his drunken and dangerous stupor?

3. Should he continue to cover for him with the legislature?

4. Should he talk with his boss's wife about the problem?

5. Should he go to the Board of Directors at the risk of losing a friend and his position?

6. How would you advise him—from an Incarnational context—to speak the truth in love?

Our Incarnate Model
"For His Glory"

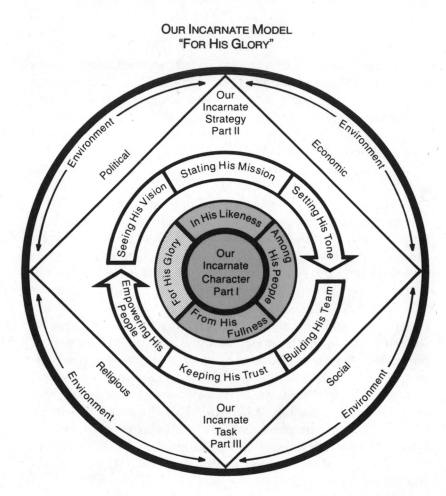

The Word became flesh and lived for a while among us. *We have seen his glory,* the glory of the one and only Son, who came from the Father, full of grace and truth.

John 1:14 NIV

6

For His Glory

To complete his profile of the Incarnate Christ, John draws again upon the Old Testament image of the Word becoming flesh and "tabernacling among us." Envision the milling masses of the Israelites trudging through the deserts, mountains and wilds of the Sinai Peninsula. In the midst of their company, they carried the "Tabernacle" or the Ark of the Covenant. From the outside, the Tabernacle appeared to be just a rough-hewn box, valuable to no one except those who built it as the temporary home for their God. Inside, however, the Israelites had inlaid pure gold with the most intricate sculpturing of the cherubim and seraphim who symbolized God's attendants in heaven. But even the pure gold paled before the "Shekinah" glory which emanated from the box. Signaling the Presence of God, the brightness of that glory blinded human eyes and struck dead those who tried to look at it. Through Moses, the Lord warned Aaron not to come into the most Holy Place behind the curtain of the Ark because the light of the "Shekinah" would kill him (Leviticus 16:2).

As holy and awesome as it was, Shekinah glory had a practical purpose. As a reminder of the Presence of God within, a cloud appeared on the Tabernacle by day and a flame by night. When the cloud lifted and began to move, the people were to move. When the cloud settled on the Tabernacle, the people were to rest. So, God's glory served as the guiding presence for the children of Israel.

The Holy-Common Paradox

When John writes, "We beheld His glory, the glory as of the Only Begotten of the Father," his first thought must have been that moment of splendor on the Mount of Transfiguration when he with Peter and James came out of his sleep and witnessed the glory of Christ, the Son of God. Such an experience only heightens the tension of the paradox that is hidden in his words. To behold the glory of God is to die. And we cannot forget the fact that Incarnation began when Jesus "emptied" Himself of His glory as the Son of God. How then do we reconcile John's words with these facts?

The Old Testament image of the Tabernacle helps us. The glory which rested on the Ark assured the Israelites of God's Presence and served as the guide for their daily march. From the beginning to the end of biblical history, we are given the assurance of divine presence in the pilgrimage of life. To Jacob, God promised:

> I am with you and will watch over you wherever you go, and I will bring you back to this land. I will not leave you until I have done what I have promised you.
>
> Genesis 28:15 NIV

Isaiah adds poetic grandeur to the promise even when Israel is disobedient and in captivity:

Fear not, for I have redeemed you; I have summoned you by name; you are mine. When you pass through the waters, I will be with you; . . . .

Isaiah 43:1b–2a

Of course, the actual Presence of Jesus Christ gave His disciples the assurance that they needed in preparation for the future. He also knew their fear of being left alone. We share that fear. So, Jesus' final word to His disciples for all ages is, "I will be with you always, to the very end of the age" (Matthew 28:20 NIV). The Word which became flesh and lived among us has that same glory of Person and proof of presence. An aura of reflective glory surrounded the life and ministry of Jesus Christ.

Another approach to understanding the Incarnate glory of the presence of Christ is to search through the many verses in which John mentions "glory" in his Gospel. Other Gospel writers usually refer to the "glory" which Christ anticipates taking up again when He returns to His Father. John does not neglect this meaning, but he puts greater emphasis upon the relationship between Father and Son. The Father glorifies the Son and the Son glorifies the Father. When Jesus resisted the temptation to divert death in His mission of salvation, His decision is framed in the conclusive words, "Father, glorify Your name." His Father answers immediately, "I have both glorified it, and will glorify it again" (John 12:27–28 NIV). So, like the Tabernacle in the wilderness, Jesus had a glory of presence among the people that could not be denied. Of this glory, He prayed that the disciples might have a share so that they might be one even as He and His Father were one (John 17:14).

The Glory of His Work

Jesus also had a glory that attended His works. When we think of Jesus' works, we tend to focus on His miracles. We cannot forget the context in which He served. The revelation of Incarnate glory came when He risked His holiness in the commonplace, among the poor and with the unclean. For example, after the miracle in which Jesus turned the water into wine at the marriage in Cana, John records:

> This, the first of his miraculous signs, Jesus performed in Cana of Galilee. He thus revealed his glory, and his disciples put their faith in him.
>
> John 2:11 NIV

Or, after entering into the tomb of Lazarus where the rancid odor of death polluted the air, Jesus says to Martha, "Did I not say to you that if you would believe you would see the glory of God?" (John 11:40).

A humbling truth confronts us. Glory that accrues to our person or our work tends to feed upon itself and become corrupted as self-glory. This explains why Jesus continued to empty Himself of His own glory. Whether in His person or His work, He gave all the glory to His Father. So, when the Jews accused Him of being a Samaritan dog and demon-possessed, Jesus invoked the test of glory, "I am not seeking glory for myself; but there is one who seeks it, and he is the judge. I tell you the truth, if a man keeps my word, he will never see death" (John 8:50 NIV). "Aha," the Jews answered, "This proves you are demon-possessed because you claim to be greater than our father Abraham who died." Jesus still held His ground, "If I glorify myself, my glory means nothing. My Father, whom you claim as your God, is the one who glorifies me" (John 8:54 NIV). Jesus let the test of glory speak for itself. By bearing God's name, obeying God's will, speaking God's Word and doing God's work, He glorified His Father in heaven.

True to His own test, when Jesus gave His final report to His Father, He reaffirmed His singular purpose to give the glory to God throughout His life. "I have brought you glory on earth by completing the work you gave me to do" (John

17:4 NIV). So the paradox of Incarnate glory is resolved. It is personal and work-related. Like the Tabernacle in the Wilderness, Jesus brought the Holy into the commonplace. Naturally, the splendor of His person and the miracle of His works would set Him apart for awe and adulation. So, to avoid the temptation to self-glory, Jesus continued to "empty" Himself of personal glory and give God the glory for whatever He said and did. Incarnate glory is reflective glory. As Jesus gave glory only to God, He promised that the Holy Spirit, in turn, would reflect only the glory of "Christ in us."

"Presence" and Leadership

We cannot deny that "presence" is an indispensable characteristic of leaders. When the military wanted to identify potential officers, they utilized all the instruments designed to sort out the personality traits and leadership styles of effective leaders. The results lacked accuracy. Either individuals or situations surprised them. Then, almost by accident, they found that the best predictor of leadership was to observe a group of persons in a room. Those individuals toward whom people moved and around whom they clustered proved to be the best candidates for future leadership. Because they did not have prior position, power or expertise that would have been known to the people who were attracted to them, the answer seemed to be a "presence" which has magnetic force.

As difficult as it is to measure the intangible quality of "presence," it cannot be ignored as a quality of Incarnate leadership. With the promise of "Christ in us" comes an integrity that sets us apart and a spirit that reflects something of His splendor. Incarnate glory is like a cosmic ray that takes a picture of a person. After the person leaves, the profile remains. So it is with Incarnate leaders. Christ's Presence is sensed when you meet them, confirmed as you get acquainted with them and it remains after they are gone.

Karsh, the photographer, revealed his genius in being able to capture the spirit of his subjects. Winston Churchill's bulldog look, Marian Anderson's beatific suffering and John Kennedy's boyish vision are portraits that equal thousands of words in their biographies. To Karsh, the secret is in the eyes and hands. But when he photographed Pablo Casals, the cellist, Karsh made an exception to his focus upon the eyes and hands. Casals is pictured in a barren, stone turret with light coming in through a small window over his head. He is hunched over his instrument with his back to the camera! When the portrait was displayed, one person kept coming back day after day to stand in silence and then leave. Curiosity prompted a curator to break his silence one day with the question. "Why do you come every day to stand in silence in front of this picture and then leave?" "Shh," the observer answered. "I'm listening to the music." Karsh caught the "presence" of the person.

Most of us react against the thought that Incarnate Christian leaders emanate an aura of glory. Part of the problem is the fact that we have swung so far from one extreme to the other. Not too many years ago, we ascribed an aura to our leaders that commanded almost idolatrous respect and blind loyalty. Charles Colson, counsel to President Nixon during the Watergate scandal, has said that he never stepped into the Oval Office without a quiver of awe. Whether it was the office or the man, Colson confessed his blind obedience in engineering the Watergate scandal. Years later, when he first returned to the White House after becoming a Christian, the quiver was gone. As Charles Colson himself would testify, he had transferred his allegiance to the Lord of lords.

We err on the other side if we assume that an Incarnational leader has no reflective glory in his or her presence. Just the fact that so many highly visible Christian leaders have abused the aura ascribed to them by people does not mean that our skepticism applies to all other leaders. Who can deny the reflective glory that is sensed in the presence and works of Mother Teresa? She is a nondescript person hardly distinguished by her gray garb. The human attributes of a "charismatic presence" are missing. Her "media presence" is limited and her interviews are undramatic. Yet, because she has taken the Holy into the commonplace, among the poor and with the unclean she has a reflective glory that attends her presence and follows her absence. Although the highest honors in the world have been heaped upon her as a sister of charity, she invariably defers the glory and gives it to God.

The Measure of Glory

If we have the likeness, mind and spirit of "Christ in us," we will be effective Incarnational leaders with a measure of glory. In fact, Jesus tied glory directly to effectiveness. In His Sermon on the Mount, He urged His followers:

> In the same way, let your light shine before men, that they may see your good deeds and praise your Father in heaven.
>
> Matthew 5:16 NIV

Later He reinforced the principle as a condition of discipleship:

> This is to my Father's glory, that you bear much fruit, showing yourselves to be my disciples.
>
> John 15:8 NIV

In these words is a warning. The temptation to glory in our good works or our spiritual fruits is ever present. Our only protection is to pursue the singular motive of the Incarnate Christ who glorified His Father. Daily, we must ask ourselves the first question in *The Westminster Shorter Catechism*, "What is the chief end of man?" and answer with captivating conviction, "Man's chief end is to glorify God and enjoy Him forever."

Glory is not hard to measure. Just a moment in the presence of a person will be the test, "Who is glorified, God or me?" The words we speak, the subjects we emphasize, the setting we create and the gleam in the eye are all tell-tale signs. Those of us who were brought up poor and powerless are particularly susceptible to self-glory. Attention flatters us and achievement bloats us. Furthermore, the "celebrity syndrome" has contagiously spread to the Christian community. Fifteen minutes of fame and we speak when we have nothing to say, write when we have nothing to write, build when we have nothing to build and take credit when the results belong to God. Self-glory has a hollow ring and false glory is repulsive.

But what a difference when we have the Presence and do the works of "Christ"—in the commonplace, among the poor and with the unclean—with an eye single to the glory of God! A maturing measure of Incarnate glory is ours when our presence leaves behind the profile of Christ and our achievements cause people to exclaim, "To God be the glory!"

C. S. Lewis sums up our thoughts with an insight that should become the prayer of every Incarnate Christian leader. In an essay on literary excellence, Lewis sees the scramble for self-glory among the authors, but then sets the Christian apart with the mind of Christ:

> Our whole destiny seems to lie in the opposite direction, in being as little as possible in ourselves, in acquiring a fragrance that is not our own, but borrowed, in becoming clean mirrors filled with an image of a face that is not ours.[1]

*   *   *

Our profile of the Incarnate Christian leader is now complete. Remembering the model of Christ's Incarnate character, we now see ourselves in His image—Figure 4:

As the "Word became flesh" in Jesus Christ, the Holy Spirit brings to birth "Christ in us." His likeness becomes our likeness; His character becomes our character; and His life becomes our life. With Him, then, we live among His people and become "servant of all"—identifying with their culture

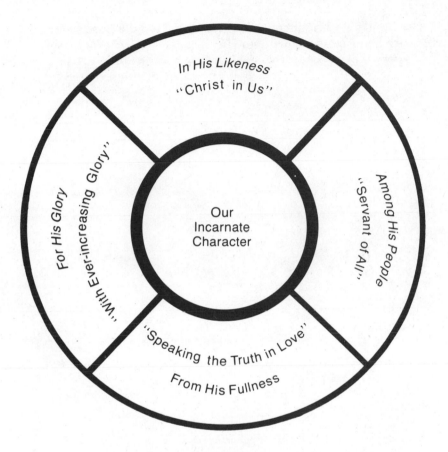

In His Likeness
"Christ in Us"

Among His People
"Servant of All"

Our
Incarnate
Character

For His Glory

"With Ever-increasing Glory"

"Speaking the Truth in Love"

From His Fullness

FIGURE 4

and responding to their needs. Accordingly, our dealings with people, whether in word or deed, have the Incarnate quality of "speaking the truth in love"—evidence of the fullness of His grace and truth. Finally, by bearing the Name of God, obeying the will of God, speaking the Word of God, and doing the work of God, we complete the cycle of "Christ in us." Our Incarnate leadership speaks for itself when our achievements are extolled, not for our glory, but for the glory of God:

And we, who with unveiled faces all reflect the Lord's glory, are being transformed into His likeness with ever-increasing glory, which comes from the Lord, who is the Spirit.

2 Corinthians 3:18 NIV

Case in Point

Within days after his release from prison, Charles Colson appeared at a conference of evangelical Christian leaders. To the surprise of many, he chain-smoked one last cigarette before taking the rostrum. As he spoke, his new language of faith got mixed up with a sprinkling of "hells" and "damns" from the vocabulary of his former self. Then, when provocative theological test questions were asked from the audience, more often than not Colson answered, "I don't know."

Since that introduction as a "born-again" celebrity, Charles Colson has grown in grace and matured in knowledge to become a respected speaker and author with both the Christian and secular publics.

About the same time, Eldridge Cleaver, the infamous head of the Black Panthers, also professed his faith in Jesus Christ. He, too, took to the lecture circuit as an evangelical celebrity. His first speeches were not unlike Colson's— sincere, but rough; articulate, but limited in religious knowledge. Not too long after his introduction, Cleaver announced other conversions, first as a Mormon and then as a Moonie. At last report, Eldridge Cleaver faced criminal charges for robbery with the likelihood of going to jail as a discredited and broken man.

1. Thomas Wolfe wrote that in our media world, everyone will be famous for five minutes. Christians suffer from the "celebrity syndrome" too. How can we recognize our celebrity converts without spoiling them as potential leaders?

2. All Christian leaders are tempted by media visibility and public attention. What has been your temptation to self-glory, even on a smaller scale than the national media? How did you handle it?

3. After Saul was converted on the Damascus Road, he spent three years in the desert before making his public appearance. Imagine that you were given the task of developing a spiritual discipline for developing him as a "celebrity convert" in his faith. What discipline and schedule would you recommend?

Part Two

Our Incarnate Strategy

OUR INCARNATE MODEL
"SEEING HIS VISION"

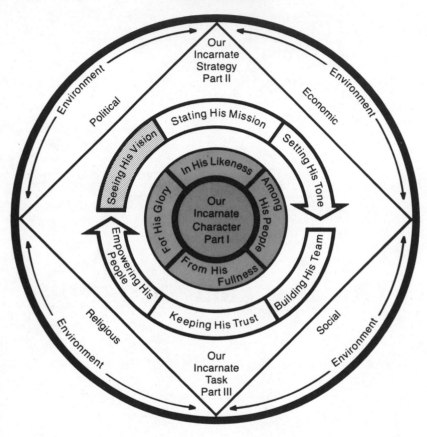

For the Son of Man came to seek and
to save what was lost.
Luke 19:10 NIV

7

Seeing His Vision

Critics accuse Jesus of being a visionary. Of course He was. Without a vision, leaders flounder and people perish. Not that every leader is a visionary pathfinder. Some leaders have special gifts of planning; others have gifts for implementing those plans and managing resources. But even in these cases, if the leaders are to be effective, their gifts will be guided by a meaningful, motivating and mobilizing vision.

In doing the research for their book *In Search of Excellence,* Peters and Waterman made a discovery about leadership in the corporate world.[1] They set out to find the best-run companies in the United States, study their qualities and identify the common factors which made them excellent. To limit the scope of their study, Peters and Waterman assumed that the margin for excellence was created by factors other than the leadership of the company. Their search proved them wrong. In each company that they identified as excellent, they also discovered a legendary leader, past or present, who had a vision for the future of the firm. While the visions varied from corporation to corporation, they all had something in common. In each case, the leader had a vision of shared values for the company along with a priority on human resources, namely the personal growth and professional development of people.

What Are We Trying to Do for Whom?

Now we know. The first responsibility of a leader is to see a vision which addresses the question, "What are we trying to do for whom?" As simple as it may sound, the answer to this strategic question will make the difference between excellence and mediocrity in an organization, as well as in its leadership.

Strategic management has become the code-word for contemporary leadership. The term "strategy," however, means different things to different people. Henry Mintzberg sees "strategy" identified in five ways.[2] First, strategy may be a *plan* of attack or action which takes its meaning from a military setting. Second, strategy may also be a *ploy* in which a specific plan of action is designed to outwit and beat an opponent. Third, strategy may be the result of a *pattern* which develops over a period of time so that the future follows the past.

Whether plan, ploy or pattern, there is a deficiency in these definitions. In each case, immediacy and expediency dictate the strategy. So, Mintzberg upgrades the definition to strategy as *position,* meaning that the organization or institution finds its place in the competitive environment and sets strategy to "match" its purpose with its position. Most strategic planning, particularly in the business and educational setting, puts heavy emphasis upon an "environment scan" in order to respond to changing needs and differentiate its position against the competition.

For Christian leaders, the definition of strategy as position is still not adequate. We need Mintzberg's fifth definition of strategy as *perspective* to rescue us from the mentality of immediacy, expediency and competition.

Strategy as *perspective* is a concept which advances the content, character and commitment of an organization as the distinctive and integrated way in which it perceives the world and responds to it. In other words, the mission of the organization determines its distinctive, not changing its environment, past patterns or threatening competition.

This does not mean that Christian organizations are insensitive to cultural changes. Periodic environmental scans are absolutely essential for churches and Christian organizations whose mission will continue to be responsive to the personal and social needs of changing times. A dynamic mission, however, does not mean knee-jerk reactions or cultural captivity.

In Mintzberg's terms, every Christian organization should be a "missionary" organization whose strategy is a distinctive and integrated *perspective* that is shared in the commitment of its members. If that perspective falters or blurs, the strategy of Christian organizations will lapse into plans, ploys, patterns and positions.

An Incarnate Christian leader has one priority task. It is to keep the strategy for the Christian organization on the razor's edge of being vision-directed, mission-minded and environmentally tuned.

Appointed to a college presidency at the green age of thirty-one, I missed the opportunity to be mentored by a senior president in higher education. So, as one of the first acts of administration at Spring Arbor College in 1961, I engaged Tom Jones, esteemed President of Earlham College, to serve as our consultant as we assessed the future for our small, two-year college, struggling to grow up and become a four-year Christian liberal arts college. The moment Tom arrived on campus he advanced the question, "What's the Big Idea?" Relentlessly, then, he drove home the point with our trustees and faculty. The future of Spring Arbor College, he said, depended upon a "Big Idea" that would focus its purpose as a Christian college and differentiate its mission in higher education.

To illustrate his point, Tom told the story of his presidential leadership at Earlham College in Indiana. He too came to the presidency of a struggling institution which needed a vision. Out of the Quaker history of the college and the dreams of the trustees and faculty, he fashioned the "Earlham Idea"—to provide a liberal arts education for a selected student body in the Quaker tradition of quality and compassion.

Once the "Earlham Idea" took root in the minds of the people, Tom Jones decided to "flesh out" its meaning by recruiting a faculty member who personified the ideal. Bold as Daniel entering a den of lions, Jones traveled to Stanford University and invited its distinguished chaplain, known for his teaching and writing, to come to Earlham. To the surprise of many and the consternation of some, Elton Trueblood responded affirmatively to the invitation. The rest is history. Earlham College is one of the nation's distinguished liberal arts colleges— shaped by a vision and personified by its leadership.

Out of the experience with Tom Jones came the "Spring Arbor Concept," the Big Idea that continues to shape that institution more than twenty-five years after its inception. Symbolized by a logo now sculpted over the fountain at the center of the campus, the Concept centers in a lamp of learning which is intersected by a cross whose stake and arms reach up, down and out to touch a global ellipse. Every student and alumnus knows the meaning of these symbols—the lamp represents involvement in the serious study of the liberal arts, the cross calls for personal commitment to Jesus Christ and the ellipse identifies the responsibility for critical participation in the contemporary world. Not unlike the Earlham idea of Tom Jones, the Spring Arbor Concept quickly gathered its critics and took time to rally its advocates. But more than twenty-five years later, the faculty will not let the Concept go as the shaping vision for its people and programs.

The Vision of Jesus

The leadership of Jesus was guided by an Incarnate vision which answered the question, "What are we trying to do for whom?" After creating a public furor by inviting Himself to dinner at the home of the hated tax-collector Zacchaeus, Jesus explained His purpose by sharing His vision:

> . . . the Son of Man came *to seek and to save what was lost.*
> Luke 19:10 NIV

Nothing more need be said. We know how Jesus answered the question, "What are we trying to do for whom?"

Jesus' leadership is focused and differentiated by this vision. It is focused upon redemption and differentiated from all other religions. Especially, in contrast with Pharisaical religion that offered little hope for the future, catered to the righteous and protected its own turf, Jesus would take the initiative to go among the lost and give them the good news of salvation. His Incarnate vision is meaningful, motivating and mobilizing.

A Meaningful Vision

The meaning of Jesus' vision is most evident when He puts it into practice. To the Samaritan woman at the well, whose birth as a half-breed and life as a profligate made her a social outcast and spiritual leper, Jesus offers the word of hope:

> For God did not send his Son into the world to condemn the world, *but to save the world through him.*
> John 3:17 NIV

Also, Jesus uses His focused vision to differentiate His ministry. In contest with the Jews, after the healing of blind Bartimaeus, Jesus wastes no words in distinguishing the meaning of His ministry:

> I am the gate; whoever enters through me will be saved. He will come in and go out, and find pasture. The thief comes only to steal and kill and destroy; I have come that they may have life, *and have it to the full.*
> John 10:9–10 NIV

A meaningful vision, then, is one that focuses attention on our primary purpose, integrates our actions and engages others as participants in an exciting and significant future. This is the real test of a leader's vision. Both the Samaritan woman and blind Bartimaeus became communicators of Jesus' redemptive plan. Enlivened by its hope and transformed by its power, they assumed a significant role as its witnesses and defenders.

A Motivating Vision

His vision "to seek" the lost gave Jesus the motive for His efforts. Early in His ministry, He faced the temptations of success and popularity. It would have been easy to locate Himself in Capernaum, establish Himself in the synagogue and let the people come to Him. The idea made sense. He would have established His identity as a teacher, conserved His energy and ministered to people who were serious enough to seek Him out. To do so, however, would betray His vision. So, against the pressure of earnest people who urged Him to stay, Jesus said:

> I must preach the good news of the kingdom of God to the other towns also, *because that is why I was sent.*
>
> Luke 4:43 NIV

His vision also served to differentiate His mission to "the lost." The religion of the Jews had deteriorated into a self-protective system for a closed circle of those who met their rigid standards of righteousness. True to the test of a dead or dying institution, their rule book got thicker and their bureaucracy became heavier. Soon, the people existed to serve the institution rather than the institution serving the people. Jesus' vision to seek and save the lost did not disturb the Jewish leadership as long as it remained verbal. But when He acted out its meaning by eating with "many tax collectors and sinners" in Levi's house, they realized the threat and questioned His motive. On hearing their criticism, Jesus restated the motive of His mission to "the lost":

> It is not the healthy who need a doctor, but the sick. I have not come to call the righteous, but sinners.
>
> Mark 2:17 NIV

A Mobilizing Vision

Unless the vision of a leader mobilizes the energies of persons and the resources of an organization, it will fail. When Warren Bennis and Burt Nanus were conducting interviews for their book, *Leaders: Strategies for Taking Charge,* they tried unsuccessfully to reach Sergiu Comissiona, Conductor of the Houston Symphony who had been commended to them as an outstanding leader. Finally, they resorted to asking members of the symphony what they thought about the leadership of Comissiona. "Terrific," the musicians answered. "But why?" the interviewers asked. The musicians wavered—perhaps attesting to the fact that a leader's vision is often more intuitive than rational. Finally, they answered, "He doesn't waste our time."[3]

Highest compliments sometimes come in plain packages that need to be unwrapped. We might think that Comissiona's musicians were damning him with the faintest of praise. "He doesn't waste our time" is not a flowery commendation. Yet, I remember one of the highest compliments paid to me after I moved from one presidential position to another. My former secretary told a friend, "The office was a pressure cooker. We often worked on the edge of panic. But we were never bored."

Jesus did not waste His disciples' time. With what Bennis and Nanus call "unbridled clarity," He set expectations which required full mobilization for the energies of His followers. In his book *No Easy Victories,* John Gardner describes the difference between the relaxed life of jet setters and the busy whirl of a leader who is striving for excellence. Jet setters wake up every morning to nothing more than the challenge of lowering their golf score or imagining an exotic theme for their next party. The leader who is striving for excellence, however, wakes up to a day in which every ". . . capacity or talent one may have is needed, every lesson one may have learned is tested, and every value one cares about is furthered."[4]

Jesus kept stretching His disciples. Each day they had to reach deep within themselves to find resources equal to their challenge. Certainly, Jesus' vision "to seek and save the lost" mobilized the best in them and their simple organization. Edwin Land, father of the Polaroid camera, describing his own visionary leadership, said, "The first thing you naturally do is teach the person that the undertaking is manifestly important and nearly impossible."[5] Energies of people and resources of organizations are mobilized by a vision that is "manifestly important and nearly impossible."

Focusing the Vision

At one time or another, most of us fret over the lack of focus in our lives. Our son, a sophomore in college, spoke of that frustration just the other day. As he felt the pressure to choose his major field of study and begin pointing toward a career, he compared his lack of focus with his older brother who has found his niche and performs with high intensity. I reminded him that the average college student changes majors three or four times during the undergraduate experience. Also, people are changing careers three and four times during their working years. But then I told him that his older brother was a late-bloomer, deciding on his major late in his college career when a professor of psychology excited him about the field. My advice was to continue building a strong foundation in the liberal arts, explore the options of vocational choice, enjoy his college years and relax in a commitment to do the full will of God. His vision will come into focus.

We will be encouraged to learn that Jesus' vision became sharper and more specific as His career advanced. This is not unusual. When leaders have been asked to speak their vision, they have no doubt about their long-term goal. But when it comes to specifics, they can only speak a short-term plan of action. If asked to state their goal three or five years into the future, for instance, they will get a playful gleam in their eye and restate their vision by telling a story or even cracking a joke. According to Peters and Waterman, legendary leaders are masters at myth-making. Experience and wisdom have taught them that a vision must be flexible in focus at the same time it is firm in purpose.

Consider the sharpening of Jesus' vision of the future in the Gospel of Mark. John the Baptist introduces Jesus with the prophetic pronouncement, "Behold the Lamb of God who takes away the sin of the world." Building upon John's introduction, Jesus opens His public ministry with the announcement, "The time has come, the kingdom is at hand, repent and believe the gospel." While there is no question that salvation is to be the theme for His ministry, Jesus relates His vision to John's call for repentance and then differentiates His ministry by advancing to the Good News of the Gospel. Through a series of ministry acts, then, Jesus establishes His servant role. The pattern of His actions reveals His strategy—healing the sick, casting out demons, forgiving sinners, debating with Pharisees, consorting with sinners, moving from town to town and teaching His disciples.

Still within the vision "to seek and save the lost," Jesus is establishing His identity as the Son of Man and servant of the people. Then, with propitious timing, He checks on His performance by asking His disciples, "Who do people say I am?" Public opinion is confused. The disciples answer, "Some say John the Baptist, others say Elijah, and still others, one of the prophets" (Mark 8:27–28 NIV). "Fair enough," Jesus seems to say, "But what about you? Who do you say that I am?" For all the disciples, Peter answers, "You are the Christ." The feedback is vital to the next step in His ministry. Having led His disciples to this insight, Jesus advances to the prediction of His death:

> He then began to teach them that the Son of Man must
> suffer many things and be rejected by the elders, chief priests
> and teachers of the law, and that he must be killed and after
> three days rise again.
>
> Mark 8:31 NIV

Jesus' vision has not changed, but the focus has been sharpened to show the necessity of His suffering, rejection, death and resurrection to save the lost. The news is more than the disciples can handle. They had bought into His vision of servanthood, but not into the vision of His suffering.

Why did Jesus wait until this time to announce His impending death? Did He not know that He must die when He began His ministry? Or did He hold the news until the disciples had enough faith in Him to work it through? If we follow the pattern of visionary leadership, the answer is that Jesus knew the risk of death, but hoped that the acceptance of His message and ministry might open another way. Events taught Him otherwise. There was no alternative. "To seek and save the lost," He had to die.

The focus of Jesus' vision gets still sharper in His second prediction of death. As He strides out in front of them on the way to certain death in Jerusalem, He tells His astonished disciples:

> . . . the Son of Man will be betrayed to the chief priests
> and teachers of the law. They will condemn him to death and
> hand him over to the Gentiles, who will mock him and spit on
> him, flog him and kill him. Three days later he will rise.
>
> Mark 10:33 NIV

In the cross hairs of His sharpening vision, Jesus now sees Judas' betrayal, Israel's condemnation, and the Gentiles' humiliation.

Against this background, Jesus restates His vision one more time. He still does not deviate from the purpose, "to seek and save the lost," but the way it will be accomplished has shifted from serving to suffering.

For even the Son of Man did not come to be served, but to serve, and to give his life as a ransom for many.

Mark 10:45 NIV

From then on, all of Jesus' words and acts take on an apocalyptic tone. An ominous and darkening cloud of death hangs heavy over His soul. His vision "to seek and save the lost" has evolved from preaching the gospel and serving the people to predicting His passion and readying Himself for death.

Our Incarnate Vision

All the principles growing out of Jesus' Incarnate vision apply to Christian leadership today. First and foremost, *we must have Christ's vision.* Every person in whom Incarnation continues will see that the primary reason for our existence is "to seek and save the lost." The vision should be engraved on every business card of Christian leaders and embroidered on every banner that flies over Christian organizations. Anything short of this Incarnate vision is sub-Christian.

When I consult with denominations, colleges and parachurch organizations that are trying to write a mission statement, I remind them of Christ's Incarnate vision. It precedes, disciplines and determines the direction for all Christians, individually or corporately. If we take that vision for granted, we risk losing the meaning, motivation and mobilization essential to Christian leadership. A self-serving vision takes over, our focus blurs and our mission statements degenerate into competitive differences. Rather than asking, "What are we trying to do for whom?" we ask, "How can we justify our existence and beat the competition?"

If, however, Christ's Incarnate vision is our vision, we find the meaning, motivation and mobilization that we need to be effective as leaders. Furthermore, our leadership takes on exciting and infinite significance as we become partners in the redemptive task of transforming people from leading selfish and sinful lives to the full satisfaction of serving people and glorifying God.

Christ's Incarnate vision is not limited to ordained positions or professional careers in ministry. Christian leaders can see the redemptive vision in any vocational field as "missionaries without portfolio"—either on an individual or institutional basis. We must never forget that Jesus came into a climate conducive to redemption. The climate had been created by the intervening influence of the Holy Spirit, the powerful words of faithful prophets, the natural cycle of human history and even the unexpected control of the Roman Empire. So, whatever we do as Incarnate leaders, whether creating a climate conducive to redemption or engaging in a specific ministry of redemption, the same vision presides over our work. Each of us is called to answer the question, "How is my leadership contributing to the redemptive vision of seeking and saving the lost?" If we are contributing nothing, we must either change our ways or our work.

Our vision must also motivate us to make a life-giving commitment. Few things are worth dying for. Yet, just as Jesus' vision came to focus upon the inevitability of His death, we cannot escape the same reality. Each night I watch news reports. Frequently, scenes are shown of "freedom fighters" across the world who leave their homes and families to do battle against insurmountable odds that minimize the chance of victory and maximize the risk of death. Yet, as they fight on, I ask myself, "For what am I willing to die?" Frankly, I do not have the answer. If pressed to the wall, I believe I would be willing to die for Christ. But to take the initiative "to seek and save the lost" at the risk of death, I shrink back into my comfort.

Before Pat Robertson declared his candidacy for the presidency of the United States, he and I talked. Picking up on our past conversations, we talked about education and evangelism. Then Pat said, "Let me ask your counsel." He proceeded to tell me how he was testing the climate to determine whether or not to run for the presidency. Just as if someone snapped on a light switch, Pat's eyes danced with inspiration. The light caught fire as he shared the conviction that God had destined him to run and win. Then, realizing that he had communicated a premature announcement, he paused and asked again for my counsel. I was smart enough to know that nothing I could say would make a difference. Pat Robertson had been set aflame by a motivating vision. Awe, envy and doubt swirled within me as I left our meeting. For the first time, I had met a person who had the motivation to change the world. How I wished that I had the same all-consuming inspiration for my leadership task. But as I closed the door behind me, I also thought, *That kind of motivation can make you a martyr!*

Our Incarnate vision must mobilize our resources—time, money, knowledge, space and especially people. In recent years, we have been blessed by an abundance of resources. Little discipline has been necessary because there is always more to replace what we have wasted. Now, having been spoiled by a spiraling growth economy, we may not be ready for a time when we must conserve and allocate limited resources in order to be both efficient and effective in achieving our goals. The discipline is exacting. If we ask whether or not we are spending our limited resources on the initiative of seeking and saving the lost rather than serving and comforting the saved, the truth hurts. If we ask whether or not salvation for the lost is the visible result of our expenditures, the sting increases. And, if we dare ask whether or not the point of action for our ministry is among the lost rather than the saved, the pain is total.

I concur with the conclusion that Buhlmann has drawn in his book, *The Coming of the Third Church.* He sees the First Church of the East as lapsed into silence, the Second Church of the West as rich in resources, but desperately in need of renewal, and the Third Church of the South and developing nations as the place where the Spirit of God is moving with dynamic power and grace.[6] According to Buhlmann, the renewal of the Second Church of the West depends upon the utilization of its resources in support of the surging spirit in the coming Third Church. Christ's Incarnate vision is uniquely ours. To save ourselves, we must give ourselves by mobilizing our resources "to seek and save the lost" at home and abroad.

Our Incarnate vision sharpens in focus as we mature. Long ago, I adopted a rule for life, "Never stand still and never go back." Having been in a two-year college, I didn't want to go back. Having taught in a public university, I didn't want to go back. Having been the president of a four-year college, I didn't want to go back. While my love for those institutions remains strong, the focus for my vision has changed. Looking forward, I find my excitement in unexplored territory.

A more profound change, however, has come into the focus of my vision. As I have moved forward into new territory, spiritual values have taken on sharper definition. I can remember when personal recognition and institutional reputation stood high on my list of needs. They were not sinful because they were kept in check by criticism, failure and the grace of God. Now, however, they have fallen behind. Seeing the Incarnate vision of Christ more clearly, I want to be identified with seeking and saving the lost, whether as a clergyman preaching the gospel or as a lay person creating a climate conducive to redemption. In either case, the questions are the same:

• Is Christ's redemptive vision exciting and significant for me?
• How am I contributing to that vision through my leadership?
• Is the vision sharpening in focus upon spiritual values as I mature?

Once we see and share His redemptive vision in these terms, we can advance our strategy to stating His mission with the precision of operational and measurable goals.

Case in Point

Servicemaster is an international and publicly owned corporation of individual franchises which specializes in custodial services for hospitals, clinics, laboratories and similar institutions. Founded by W. L. Wade and followed in the Chairmanship by Kenneth Hansen and Kenneth Wessner, Servicemaster has been led throughout its history by Christians whose integrity and stature are recognized in both the corporate and Christian worlds. Faithfully, they have articulated this vision for Servicemaster which greets all visitors to their corporate offices:

SERVICEMASTER

Our Vision

To be an ever expanding and vital market vehicle for use by God to work in the lives of people as they serve and contribute to others.

1. Is this vision meaningful, motivating and mobilizing?
2. Does it integrate a Christian commitment with business principles?
3. What about the individual franchises in the field? How can the vision be communicated and implemented among persons who are not Christians? What would you do if your individual franchisers achieve the market goal of the vision at the expense of the ministry to people?
4. Can you state a one sentence vision for your organization? Is it meaningful, motivating and mobilizing for you and your people?

OUR INCARNATE MODEL
"STATING HIS MISSION"

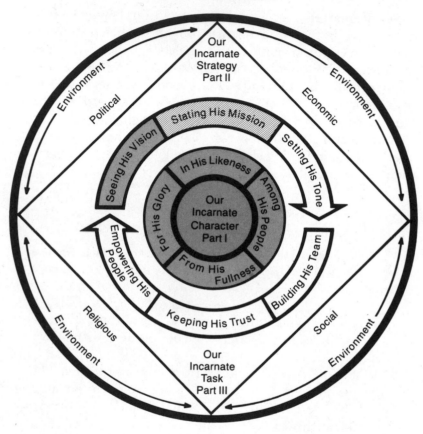

> *The Spirit of the Lord is on me, because he has anointed me to preach good news to the poor.* He has sent me to proclaim freedom for the prisoners and recovery of sight for the blind, to release the oppressed, to proclaim the year of the Lord's favor.
>
> Luke 4:18–19 NIV

8

Stating His Mission

Mission follows vision in the strategy of Incarnation. Whereas the redemptive vision focuses upon the question "Why?", the mission statement emphasizes "How?" Whereas the redemptive vision is exciting and significant, the mission statement must be operational and measurable. Not that they conflict. Vision and mission must always be consistent and complementary. The vision inspires the mission and the mission implements the vision.

Criteria for Mission

Students of leadership have certain criteria for judging an operational and measurable mission statement. The consultants of McKinsey and Company, for instance, have identified seven components of a mission statement. All begin with "S":

STRUCTURE:	Plan of the organization
STRATEGY:	Actions in the external environment

Systems:	Processes in the internal environment
Staff:	Specialties of the members
Skills:	Capabilities of the organization and its staff
Style:	Leadership patterns of senior executives
Shared Values:	Spiritual or philosophical principles to be instilled in its members

Peters and Waterman call "Structure and Strategy" the "hardware" of an organization and the other five factors the "software."[1] Rightfully, critics complain that management theory has concentrated its attention on the "hardware" to the neglect of the "software." The tide is turning. Much more attention is being given to research on the systems, staff, skills, style and shared values or the "culture" of organizations. Effective leaders will neglect neither the "hardware" nor the "software" when they state their mission for the organization.

Jesus stated His mission in the inaugural sermon that He gave in the synagogue at Capernaum. True to His vision "to seek and save the lost," He chose the prophecy of Isaiah as His text:

> The Spirit of the Lord is on me, because he has anointed me to preach good news to the poor. He has sent me to proclaim freedom for the prisoners and recovery of sight for the blind, to release the oppressed, to proclaim the year of the Lord's favor.
>
> Luke 4:18–19 NIV

Within these words are all the criteria for a mission statement in our incarnational strategy. The criteria apply to any Christian leadership role.

Following alliterative style as an aid to memory and understanding, Jesus' mission statement from the prophecy of Isaiah includes:

| Mandate: | His authority for leadership |
| Medium: | His method of operation |

MESSAGE: His content for communication
MARKET: His field for work
MEASURE: His goals for effectiveness
MOOD: His keynote for change

Jesus' Mandate for Mission. The Holy Spirit continues to shape the Incarnate leadership of Jesus. We remember that Incarnation was an act of the Holy Spirit as He fathered Jesus through whom "the Word became flesh." We also remember the affirmation of the Father when the Spirit settled upon Him like a dove and God spoke, "You are My Beloved Son in Whom I am well-pleased." Now, Jesus informs us that He has been appointed and anointed by the Holy Spirit. This is His sanctification. Jesus is "set apart" for a holy task.

Jesus' Medium for Mission. Many options were open to Jesus. He had gifts for preaching, teaching, counseling, debating, healing and exorcism. During the course of time, He proved that He had political savvy and economic understanding by which He might have sought to change the system. Furthermore, He appealed to the rich and poor, the young and old, the Jew and the Greek. Sound strategy, however, requires an assessment of personal strengths and weaknesses in order to maximize leadership effectiveness. Jesus may well have chosen preaching as the medium for His mission, not just because of His knowledge of truth and His skill in communication, but also because preaching minimized His weaknesses.

What were those weaknesses? They were the disadvantages of limited time and presence. Jesus knew that He did not embark on a long-term mission. Sooner or later, His opposition would become so threatened that they would stop at nothing to rid the world of Him. With the inevitability of death came an urgency. Jesus had to choose the means by which He could reach the largest number of people in the shortest period of time.

The mission of Jesus also had global proportions but He could only be in one place at a time. So, He chose preaching as the means of mass communication to sow the seeds of the gospel and set the pattern for world-wide evangelism. Through preaching He hoped to multiply Himself in the diversity and dispersion of His disciples. Turning weakness into strength, Jesus chose preaching as the strategic method for His mission in order to: (1) reach as many people as possible in the shortest period of time and (2) set the pattern for world evangelization.

Jesus' Message for Mission. As might be expected, Jesus had only one message—the Good News of the gospel. Rigorously, even brutally, He disciplined Himself to avoid the tangents of political and social issues that would have diverted Him from His message. How wise He was. Only the Good News of God has the substance of truth and the Spirit of grace which is the essence of communication for the Incarnation. Throughout His ministry He reinforced this message by speaking with assurance, "Truly, truly, I say unto you . . . ." Whenever He uttered these words, the veil of revelation lifted:

. . . promising the truth sets us free (John 8:32),
. . . identifying Himself as the way, the truth and the life (John 14:6), and
. . . tying His message to His mission, "I came to testify to the truth" (John 18:37).

Keep in mind, it is only when the truth is tempered by grace through the work of the Holy Spirit that the "Good News" of the gospel is communicated. Jesus' message of "Good News" is inseparable from His Incarnational traits—grace and truth.

Television news has created a problem for modern communication. Through the instant relay of news scenes, our minds are engaged in the violence, tragedy and suffering of people around the world. But because television only announces the news in time slots of thirty to sixty seconds, the scene passes without analysis of the problem and without showing us how we can help with the solution. Consequently, we become alert, but detached, observers of "bad news." Television producers are aware of the dilemma they create. So, they hire attractive, upbeat personalities to report the news and plan the newscasts to finish with a "good news" note—a human interest story, a musical postlude or a sunset. Still, the "bad news" image persists. Television news creates compassion without commitment or, we might say, it separates truth from grace and leaves us with our heads detached from our hearts. Only the message of the gospel makes us whole as well as free.

Jesus' Market for Mission. The mandate, medium and message are background for Jesus' specific goals of ministry. No one can accuse Him of being an idealist without an operational plan. When He announces the "poor" as His priority, He reveals that His ministry will be responsive to those who are needy and ready for the Good News. Rather than fighting through the barriers of those who are powerful, rich and righteous, His limited time requires a selective market for His ministry.

The decision to give the "poor" priority shows that Jesus not only identified with the people of His culture but also assessed the threats and opportunities of its environment. Strategic planners ask "WOT'S up?" when they develop a Mission Statement. "WOT'S up?" is an acronym for assessing "Weaknesses, Opportunities, Threats and Strengths." Weaknesses and strengths refer to the person who is the leader and the organization which is led; threats and opportunities relate to the environment in which the leader must work. Earlier, we noted the strengths and weaknesses of Jesus' leadership that led Him to choose preaching as the medium for His message. Now, in His decision to center His ministry among the "poor" we see the results of an environmental assessment of threats and opportunities.

Jesus' first objective of ministry with the "poor" was to "proclaim freedom for the captives." Roman legions ruled the *political environment* of Jesus' day with a mailed fist of intimidation, imprisonment and crucifixion as their way of keeping the peace. Either physical or psychological chains "bound" the people of Israel. Always a proud and free nation, they were haunted by the humiliation of Roman rule. While Jesus categorically rejected the idea that He advocated political revolution, His goal was to set people free from the political chains that bound them. Even in prison, they would be more free than their captors.

Jesus' second objective with the "poor" was to "heal the brokenhearted" (Isaiah 61:1). Although the text varies between Isaiah and Luke, the ministry of Jesus reinforces the fact that the "brokenhearted" were people who were victims of the *economic environment.* Prolonged poverty makes "broken" people. The nation of Israel had a locked-in system of extreme wealth and abject poverty that was sustained by political corruption and religious insensitivity. "Brokenness" comes from the futility of having no escape from poverty.

In the book *Rachel and Her Children,* a true story of the homeless in America, the victims of poverty describe their plight by saying, "I can't breathe."[2] Then, in the same breath, they curse God and ask His forgiveness. After rejection at every turn, they sink into the futility of having no escape. Rachel says that she would sell her body to free her children. Those of us who would condemn her do not have the mind and heart of Jesus. He would identify with her "brokenness" and give Himself to her healing.

The third objective of Jesus in giving priority to the poor is to "release the oppressed." Having lived among the people of Israel, Jesus knew personally the oppressive threat of the *social environment.* Other versions of Scripture translate the word "oppressed" as the "bruised." There is a difference between being "broken" and being "bruised." Economic oppression breaks people by futility; social oppression bruises people with discouragement. Bruised people still have hope, but they lack the courage to go on. The "bruised" of Jesus' day included widows, orphans, divorcees, lepers, epileptics, Samaritans, prostitutes, tax collectors, the handicapped and children. In each case, the stigma of society had bruised their self-esteem so badly that they felt dehumanized. Jesus, who made Himself nothing in the Incarnation, identified with the "bruised" and encouraged them to go on.

Finally, Jesus assesses the threat to the "poor" from the *religious environment,* the very sector from which freedom from oppression and hope for the future should come. Instead, He chose the word "blind" to describe the spiritual condition of the people who have been victimized by the Pharisees and their oppressive demands for righteousness. Rejecting the Word of their own prophets and resisting the movement of the Holy Spirit which brought Christ to earth, they closed their eyes to the truth to protect the religious system they had concocted. No oppression is as brutal or unfair as spiritual oppression. Like propagandists who manipulate information to control people, the Pharisees purposefully kept the poor "blind" to the truth. Worse yet, they actually justified and fortified the political, economic and social oppressors by offering no freedom for the "bound," no healing for the "broken" and no encouragement for the "bruised."

Political, economic, social and religious oppression combined to pose the greatest threat to Jesus' mission. Ordinarily, they were archenemies of each other. But when they joined in an unholy coalition, Jesus knew that they could put Him on a cross. Despite this fact, Jesus turned the threats into opportunities.

Jesus' Measure for His Mission. After specifying the "bound, broken, bruised and blind" as His priority for ministry, He boldly and publicly announced goals that could be measured.

. . . for the bound, the goal is *freedom,*
. . . for the broken, the goal is *healing,*
. . . for the bruised, the goal is *encouragement,*
. . . for the blind, the goal is *sight.*

As proof of the measurability of Jesus' goals, when John the Baptist languished in prison under a death sentence, He sent his disciples to Jesus with the question, "Are you the one who is to come or should we look for another?" Even John the Baptist had doubts. Jesus did not answer the question directly. Instead, He sent back the word to John,

> Go back and report to John what you hear and see: the blind receive sight, the lame walk, those who have leprosy are cured, the deaf hear, the dead are raised and the good news is preached to the poor.
>
> Matthew 11:4–5 NIV

The proof is in the transformed lives of the poor. John the Baptist knew the word of the prophet Isaiah and had received the promise of the Messiah. His doubts, however, disappeared when Jesus called his attention to the results of His preaching. John bowed under the executioner's blade with the assurance that he had been chosen to announce the coming of Christ. As briefly as he lived and preached, John the Baptist died praising God.

Jesus' Mood for Mission. To communicate the keynote for His ministry, Jesus adopted an Old Testament celebration called "The Year of Jubilee." When Moses received the Law on Mount Sinai, the Lord also commanded him:

> Consecrate the fiftieth year and proclaim liberty throughout the land to all its inhabitants. It shall be a jubilee for you.
>
> Leviticus 25:10 NIV

Elaborate instructions follow. After seven cycles of sabbatical years have gone by, a trumpet is to be sounded on the day of atonement to signal the Year of Jubilee. In this fiftieth year, all the land that has exchanged hands is to be redeemed and returned to its original owner (Leviticus 25:14–34). Likewise, all Israelites who have become slaves are to be set free (25:35–55). God has good reasons for these actions. He wants to remind His people that they are not the owners of the land, only stewards. Also, He wants to remind them that they are not the owners of people, only servants.

The spiritual lesson of the Year of Jubilee is even more important. When the trumpet sounds on the day of atonement, God lets His people know that He is a God of grace who desires liberty for all His people. Spiritual freedom comes, not when we gain control over property or people, but when we depend exclusively on God as stewards of His land and servants of His people. For the Israelites who heard Jesus proclaim the Year of Jubilee as the mood for His Mission, they knew immediately that He spoke of atonement, liberty and grace—the unmerited favor of God.

In full cycle, then, we see how Jesus' vision "to seek and save the lost" takes on specific objectives which were operational and measurable. The inspiration of the vision is not lost, but implementation of the mission is now possible.

Stating Our Mission

Key questions arise from the Incarnational Mission Statement of Jesus. They serve as a guide for all Christian leaders who have a responsibility to state the mission for their organization and their followers.

1. *Is our Mission Statement consistent with our vision?* Our vision both inspires and disciplines our mission. Like pulling threads through a piece of fabric, every component of Jesus' mission contributes to the grand design of seeking and saving the lost. Christian leaders are, first of all, integrators. In stating our mission we must make sure that it is consistent with our vision. Furthermore, Christian leaders are evaluators. Our mission statements must be periodically reviewed to make sure that our plans, policies, programs, people and priorities are still contributing to that vision.

2. *Is our Mission Statement operational and measurable?* The inspiration and idealism of our redemptive vision is not lost when we state our mission. Nor is the "Why?" lost in the "How?"—which can be the temptation of technology and the bane of bureaucracy. At the same time, when we move from communicating our vision to stating our mission, the

102 ~ OUR INCARNATE STRATEGY

goals of the mission must be so specific that their operation is inferred and their outcomes are measurable. Otherwise, the mission statement can blur out into an idealism of its own and lose its critical point of accountability.

3. *Does our Mission Statement identify our spiritual authority?* Just as Jesus was sanctified or "set apart" for His holy task, Incarnate Christian leaders must be sure of their appointing and anointing by the Holy Spirit. Sanctification is in natural sequence for the work of the Holy Spirit. After the likeness of Christ is born in us and we see His redemptive vision the next logical step is to be "set apart" for a holy task in our strategic mission. With the disciples in the upper room, we need our Pentecost.

4. *Does our Mission Statement specify the medium for our message?* One of the qualities of leaders identified by Bennis and Nanus in their book *Leaders: The Strategies for Taking Charge,* is a realistic assessment of their strengths and weaknesses.[3] They lead with their strengths and learn from their weaknesses. Delegation is often necessary to compensate for weaknesses. In Jesus' case we have seen that He minimized His weaknesses of time and presence by delegating to His disciples the responsibility for the long-term and world-wide preaching of the gospel.

Our strengths and weaknesses will differ. While preaching is still the primary medium for proclaiming the gospel, when Jesus gave His disciples the Great Commission, He did not specify the medium for their message but left open the full range of gifts for going into all the world, making disciples of all nations and teaching them to obey everything that He had commanded them. Later, the apostle Paul outlined a full range of spiritual skills—from apostleship to administration—that contribute to the building of the body of Christ, the work of ministry and the edification of believers (Ephesians 4:12–13). When the Holy Spirit sets us apart for our holy task, He will also assist us in discovering and developing the medium for our message.

5. *Does our Mission Statement express the truth with grace?*
"Good news" is an announcement. Not unlike television news reports, analysis-in-depth must come from another medium, such as teaching and counseling. Still, in its own right, the message must be true to the Word of God and expressive of His grace. Incarnation continues in our message. Wherever and whenever a Christian leader speaks, the "fullness of grace and truth" must be heard. "Good news" is that message balanced and whole.

6. *Does our Mission Statement select the market for our ministry?* Cultural or environmental assessment is essential to Incarnational strategy. We too must find our mission among the "poor" who are bound, broken, bruised and blind. Yet, they may not always appear to be politically, economically, socially and spiritually impoverished. While on sabbatical at a desert resort, my wife and I discovered just how "poor" and "lost" people who are "first" with the "most" can be. Successive marriages interspersed by temporary relationships is the mode of life among most of the people whom we met. Their children are grasping for love, searching for stability and playing with morals. When a woman asked me about our family, I spoke with pride about our four children, their marriages, achievements, Christian commitments and, of course, their nine children whose pictures bulge Grandpa's billfold. She blinked her eyes, shook her head and said, "It's so unusual to hear a good story."

Incarnate leadership will always seek out the "poor"—whether the down and out or the up and out—as the market for mission. There is the danger of getting too far away from the needs of our people. Whether it is "management by walking around" among the people of our organization or going directly into the field to be among those whom we serve, our strategy must include continuous monitoring of the needs and readiness of those whom business calls "customers," management consultants call "stakeholders," religious institutions call "constituents" and Jesus calls "the poor."

7. *Does our Mission Statement include the goal of measurable change?* With every segment of the "poor" to whom Jesus ministered, He set the goal of a measurable change in people. The "bound" will be free; the "broken" will be healed; the "bruised" will be encouraged to go on; and the "blind" will receive their sight. When all is said and done, the only justifiable goal for leadership is to see a positive change in the outlook and behavior of people. Some might accuse Jesus of working only with the symptoms of oppressive systems. He had a choice. The masses of Israel wanted to make him king. Rebels against Rome stood ready to take up arms under His leadership. Even His disciples had to struggle with frustrated dreams and ambitions when He announced that His kingdom was not of this world or that He would save the lost and free the oppressed by death on a cross.

The limits of time may have affected Jesus' choice between symptoms and systems. Or, more specifically, He may have made His choice between redeeming people and reforming institutions. Entrenched and mutually reinforcing political, economic, social and religious institutions as well as the systems they create required a revolution that would have absorbed all His time and energy. And, after the revolution, what? The "poor" might be free from external oppression, but still enslaved in Spirit.

Jesus knew that the person who is redeemed from sin cannot be enslaved. When Jesus said, "You shall know the truth, and the truth shall set you free," He had more than freedom from sin in mind. People of the truth are an ever-present threat to oppression of any kind. The American Revolution of 1776 is an example. Among its roots was the Great Awakening of the 1740s. Spiritual freedom stoked the fires for political freedom.

So, while Incarnational leadership will not avoid the issues of justice in political, economic and social systems, spiritual liberty for persons comes first. The results are measurable and the ripple effect through society has proven to be renewal, reformation and, sometimes, as the last resort, revolution.

8. *Does our Mission Statement carry the keynote of hope?*
When Jesus chose the Year of Jubilee as the symbol for His
ministry, He restored the hope of the "poor." Landless and
powerless, they had no self-esteem and no promise of its
restoration in the future. Imagine, then, how they heard
Jesus' announcement of the Year of Jubilee. The vicious cycle of futility was broken. Remembering God's promise,
they could look forward to the day when they would again
be stewards of the land of their fathers and servants only of
God. No wonder the masses celebrated the coming of Jesus.
For the first time in their lives, they heard the bells of freedom ring.

Our affluent society not only has its own kind of poverty,
but also its own kind of hopelessness. Young people, for
instance, are geared to live recklessly in the present moment. Project that same attitude into the future; their vision
blurs and their hope sags. Either pessimism or numbness
prevails. Middle-aged people in their late thirties and early
forties are not much different. As "yuppies" grow older,
they face the reality of aging, but still cannot make long-
term investments in pension plans because the future is so
uncertain. So, an air of pessimism underlies our giddy sense
of well-being. Solid hope is missing. Not unlike our "poor"
counterparts in the first century, we too need the Year of
Jubilee for our day when the roots represented by land and
freedom are restored.

The key, of course, is to recognize that we cannot own land
or people. God is the sole owner. To fix our dependence
upon either the ownership of land or people is sin. We need
to acknowledge Jesus Christ as the Lord of our lives as well as
the Savior of our souls. When we do, our mission takes on
an Incarnational mood—to be stewards of all material gifts
and servants of God alone. Leaders, especially, need to give
thanks for the gifts that God has entrusted to them and, at
the same time, hold them lightly.

Our Incarnational strategy, then, includes a mission statement as a responsibility of leadership. It is different in kind

as well as degree from all other mission statements because it is Incarnational in nature. Its mandate is sanctification, its medium is preaching, its message is the gospel, its market is the poor, its measure is healing and its mood is hope. Thus, the cycle is complete. The "accountability loop" returns to our Incarnational vision which is "to seek and save the lost."

While the context of Jesus' mission statement is specially related to His ministry, the principles hold for Incarnate leaders in any setting. We must state our mission and set strategic goals in terms consistent with our vision, operational and measurable in practice, responsive and balanced in relationships, transforming and hopeful for those whom we serve. All or none of this is possible, depending upon one central and underlying truth for Incarnate leaders. We must be "set apart" to lead and serve under the anointing of the Holy Spirit.

Case in Point

Word, Incorporated, is a corporation similar to Servicemaster in the purpose of integrating Christian convictions with sound business principles. Founded by Jarrell McCracken as a company producing Christian music and recordings, Word expanded to book publishing and video production in later years. The American Broadcasting Corporation (ABC), a public corporation, bought out Word with the commitment to maintain the integrity of its mission. Later, ABC merged with Cap Cities. And still later, ABC brought in its own top management while retaining second-level executives who were part of the original team and family. Though the company is in transition, the mission statement is still intact:

WORD, INCORPORATED

Is a service company in the business of Christian communication. The goal of Word, Inc., is to enrich the lives of consumers through exemplification, life-application and communication of the Christian Gospel through various media:

— by sustaining a position of enabling, servant leadership to the evangelical community,

— by adopting and maintaining a leadership position as a publisher to the broader fellowship of believers and would-be believers, and

— by maintaining a level of profitability and return on investment sufficient to attract further capital for our future growth and financial stability.

1. Analyze the mission statement of Word, Inc. Does it state the fundamental purpose of the company, its underlying theme, its market, its resources, its comparative advantage and its goals?

2. Is the vision of Word, Inc. inherent in this mission statement? Can you state the vision in one sentence?

3. Is the mission statement for your organization as specific as the mission statement of Word, Inc.? Does it meet the criteria for implementation in day-to-day operations? Does it answer the question, "What business are we in?" Does it point to your desired future as well as your existing state?

OUR INCARNATE MODEL
"SETTING HIS TONE"

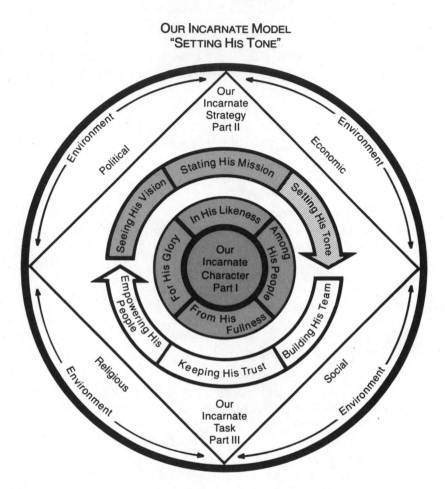

> If you obey my commands, you will re-
> main in my love, just as I have obeyed
> my Father's commands and remain in
> his love. *I have told you this so that my joy*
> *may be in you and that your joy may be*
> *complete.*
>
> John 15:10–11 NIV

9

Setting His Tone

After seeing the vision and stating the mission, leaders have a responsibility for setting the tone for their organization and for their followers. A Christian leader sets an Incarnational tone which is distinct from all others. In His inaugural address, Jesus deliberately chose tonal words:

. . . *good news* for the poor,
. . . *freedom* for the prisoner,
. . . *healing* for the broken,
. . . *release* for the oppressed,
. . . *sight* for the blind, and of course
. . . the *Year of Jubilee.*

These words of hope, however, are only a prelude to the chord of joy which He struck as the keynote for His life and ministry.

The Paradox of Joy

"Joy" is a biblical word and a spiritual concept that cannot be duplicated, falsified or mimicked in either humanistic or secular terms. "Happiness" is a human attempt to approach joy, but falls far short of its supernatural dimensions. By definition, happiness is the product of good luck or fortune. "Delight" is an emotion of extreme satisfaction that comes closer to the meaning of joy, but again its meaning tends to get tied to gratification or success. Joy has a meaning of its own.

On the divine side of the ledger, Jesus knew the *pure joy* of heaven before His Incarnation. The author of Hebrews tells us that in anticipation of knowing the "pure joy" once again, He endured the cross and scorned its shame (Hebrews 12:2). On the human side, Jesus spoke of the *practical joy* that He experienced from obeying the will and doing the work of His Father (John 15:11). In the Incarnation the two worlds come together. The *pure joy* of being in the Presence of God is joined with the *practical joy* of doing His will on earth. The result is *Incarnate joy,* a gift of the Holy Spirit which sets the tone for Jesus' redemptive vision and servant mission.

The Reward of Joy

Rewards are essential to any task. In the corporate world, salary, status and security are used as rewards as well as punishment. If granted, they are rewards; if denied, they are punishments. Peter Drucker, the father of modern management, warns against the use of money as the primary reward for our work. It is too temporary, too greedy and too corrupting, he says. Personal satisfaction, according to Drucker, is a reward of higher value. It is no secret. Satisfied workers will not only achieve more and better results, but they will also feel better about themselves and relate better to their co-workers.

Incarnate joy is spiritual satisfaction. A precise definition eludes us as it did the apostle Peter when he wrote about "inexpressible and glorious joy." We come closer to a definition when Jesus talked about His Incarnate joy. He invariably linked it with His work on earth:

. . . to *bear* the name of God,
. . . to *obey* the will of God,
. . . to *speak* the word of God, and
. . . to *do* the work of God.

This is the context in which Jesus informed His disciples, "I have told you this so that my joy may be in you and that your joy may be complete" (John 15:11 NIV).

Make no mistake. Incarnate joy is not an end in itself. C. S. Lewis learned the frustration of seeking joy and working for it as a goal. As he pursued a sense of joy down every human avenue, he confessed that he only found the traces where joy had been. Not until he sought the goal of Christ and Christ alone did he discover joy; and then it came, not by design, but by surprise. Lewis' experience teaches us that tone-setting cannot be an end in itself. Incarnate joy is an unsought "fringe benefit" of focusing upon Christ's redemptive vision and following His servant ministry.

Another distinction of Incarnate joy is its independence of circumstances. Happiness is conditional. The sensation rises or falls based upon external factors which are out of our control. Incarnate joy, however, depends only upon our obedience to the will, Word and work of God. How else can we explain the response of John the Baptist when his disciples became jealous because the masses were leaving John and going to Jesus? John said:

> The bride belongs to the bridegroom. The friend who attends the bridegroom waits and listens for him, and is full of joy when he hears the bridegroom's voice. That joy is mine, and it is now complete.
>
> John 3:29 NIV

The mystery of Incarnate joy deepens when Peter encourages Christians who are being persecuted:

> . . . rejoice that you participate in the sufferings of Christ, so that you may be overjoyed when his glory is revealed.
>
> 1 Peter 4:13 NIV

Incarnate joy ranges from the high privilege of doing the work of God to the highest privilege of sharing in Christ's suffering. Paul testifies, ". . . in all our troubles my joy knows no bounds" (2 Corinthians 7:4 NIV).

Notice again that the Holy Spirit is the instrument for the Incarnational experience of joy. Just as the Holy Spirit fathers the likeness of "Christ in us," shows us His redemptive vision and manages our servant mission, He rewards our work with the gift of joy. After the seventy-two persons whom Jesus appointed and sent out ahead of Him to preach and heal returned with the exuberant report, "Lord, even the demons submit to us in your name," He warned them not to rejoice because demons obey them, but because their names were written in heaven. Then we read:

> At that time Jesus, *full of joy through the Holy Spirit,* said, "I praise you, Father, Lord of heaven and earth, because you have hidden these things from the wise and learned, and revealed them to little children. Yes, Father, this was your good pleasure."
>
> Luke 10:21 NIV

The text teaches us that Jesus found His greatest joy when others successfully preached the Word of God and did the work of God. Confirmation, however, came as a gift of the Holy Spirit.

Incarnate joy, then, is a spiritual satisfaction that is intrinsic in value, independent of circumstances and given by the Holy Spirit as the reward for doing God's will, receiving His Word and doing His work. In our responsibility as tone-setters, we will be blessed and surprised by the "Note of Joy" that surrounds our role and our work.

The Genius of Joy

Tom Jones, the President of Earlham College, introduced me to the "Big Idea" in my first college presidency. Lewis Mayhew, Professor of Higher Education at Stanford University, taught me about the spirit behind the idea in my second presidency at Seattle Pacific University. Rapid growth over a period of years had created a financial deficit and proliferated the curriculum. To grapple with the problems we needed to refocus our vision and redefine our mission. Three prominent persons in American higher education were called in as consultants. Each spent a week on the campus becoming acquainted with our people and our programs. At the end of the week, then, they reported to a task force representing key stakeholders in the future of the institution.

In the opening interview Lewis Mayhew revealed his perspective. Without apology or arrogance, he simply said, "I am a secular humanist and I will look at Seattle Pacific through those eyes." Fair enough. As Ralph Waldo Emerson wrote, "Critics are the unpaid guardians of my soul." After a week on campus, Dr. Mayhew returned to my office for a preview of the report that he would make to the all-university task force. Equally open and honest, he said, "I have been with you for a week now. I must confess that I am still not sure what you mean in your catalog statement when you say that you are an 'evangelical Christian college.' But I do know this, if you are what you say you are, your campus will be characterized by *a note of joy!*"

Spirit and substance came together in a new vision for my leadership. Lewis Mayhew's "Note of Joy" joined Tom Jones' "Big Idea" as the energizing force for my presidency. From then on, whenever and wherever I spoke of my vision for the college, it was placed in a setting of "celebration" which expressed our note of joy as a Christian community set apart for a holy task. I shall forever be grateful for the insight of a self-professed secular humanist who saw through our vision and mission as a Christian college to the tone which all the world expects to hear.

Contagious Joy

In a reckless moment, I asked a group of five new faculty members who had just completed their first semester of teaching at Asbury Theological Seminary, "If you were president, what is the first thing you would do?" Sound suggestions that required copious notes came from the first four faculty members who spoke. Then in his turn, Dr. William Goold, Professor of Music, spoke with a devilish little twinkle in his eyes, "I'd study the law of gravity." My puzzled look caused him to continue. "In an institution like ours, the spirit of the place trickles down from top to bottom. That's why, if I were president, I'd be a student of the law of gravity."

Dr. Goold's analogy is reinforced by studies of leadership. Even though we think we are past the days when institutions were the length and shadow of its leadership, we cannot ignore the fact that leaders still significantly shape the personality of their organizations. More often than not, tone is the tip-off to that personality.

A renowned architect once said that he designed his buildings around the entrance. He meant that the first impression upon entry set the tone for the whole building.

Since then, I pay particular attention to "entry points" in organizations as well as buildings. For instance, on a recent visit to a foundation office, I had to climb over the clutter of stacked envelope boxes to lean over a high counter and tap my fingers to get the attention of a gum-chewing secretary. Immediately, I visualized chaos throughout the building and among its leadership. The whole place was dowdy, from the maze of narrow corridors to offices without personality and finally to an executive who pretended to preside over the clutter.

Talk about tone-setting at entry points! A father in our community got a nighttime call from the police informing him that his son had been in a crushing auto accident that left him trapped inside the car for forty-five minutes before being extricated by the "jaws of life." At last report, he hung between life and death when a helicopter airlifted him to the trauma center. With no further information, the father and mother sped fifteen miles through thirteen green traffic lights to the hospital. At the emergency desk, the father asked for his son and got the answer, "We don't have no Mark Wiggam. We have only a John Doe. Do you know any body marks to identify him?" In the split second before panic hit the mother, a nearby nurse heard the conversation and rescued them by pointing, "He's down there." The son lived but the insensitive response of the receptionist still ties their stomachs up in sickening knots.

By way of contrast, a high-tech company that began as a family venture gathered a team of young executives who shared the values of its original leadership. Consequently, over two or three generations, the company still has a sense of family among its members even though they employ tens of thousands in a multibillion-dollar, global business. To walk into their executive offices is an experience. Security badges which tend to depersonalize people are required. But instead of making you feel like a number, the receptionists know how to make the process human by adding a touch of humor.

One step into the office of the chief executive officer reveals the secret. The office is a warm reflection of his personality which puts you at ease as he points with pride at pictures which trace the history of the firm and plaques which honor the community spirit of the employees. Then, you learn that he has roots in the founding family of the corporation. Not blood roots, but shared values which each new generation of leadership has reinforced.

At present, the company is in transition. The last of the leaders with a commitment to the family have retired. They are being replaced by experts in corporate management, but newcomers to the culture and its values. Students of leadership are watching to see how the personality and tone of the company may be reshaped by Pharaohs "who know not Joseph."

Joy is contagious. In His high-priestly prayer just before entering into His passion, Jesus prayed earnestly that His disciples might know the joy He shared with His Father. He could give them His name, teach them His Word and show them His love, but He could not give them joy. At best, Jesus could only pray that His spiritual delight in obeying God's will, speaking God's Word and doing God's work would be contagious. No leader can manufacture joy. Just as it eludes us if we pursue it as a goal, joy will expose us if we treat it like a commodity. Our only assurance of joy is to obey God's will, speak God's Word and do God's work.

The Oil of Joy

Incarnate joy is the healing balm for Christian leadership. In the Epistle to the Hebrews, Jesus is introduced as the Son of whom God says:

> You have loved righteousness and hated wickedness; therefore God, your God, has set you above your companions *by anointing you with the oil of joy.*
>
> Hebrews 1:9 NIV

Joy distinguished Jesus. Because He obeyed God, He received the anointing of the oil of joy which set Him above His companions, or better said, caused them to look up to Him.

Firms that engage in the search for executives are ungraciously called "head hunters." When they come down to the finalists for a position, they begin to look for the "flair factor" among the candidates. They ask, "Assuming that all other things are equal among the finalists, what is the distinguishing factor that we seek?" That factor may be style, expertise, image or character. Once the "flair factor" is identified, the choice can usually be made.

"Joy" is the flair factor for Christian leadership. It reveals so much about the person. Joy attends the vision of redemption; joy results from the mission of servanthood; and joy sets the tone for implementing the Incarnational strategy.

Before moving to Asbury Theological Seminary as President, I was granted a sabbatical month at Cambridge University by the Board of Trustees of Seattle Pacific University. I wanted to read primary sources in Wesleyan history. John Wesley's leadership style particularly intrigued me. As a bonus for the experience, I met a young doctoral candidate named Tom Albin who had already done extensive research in the Wesley archives. Tom served as a walking compendium of Wesleyana—knowing the key sources, steering me away from duplications, conversing with me about my reading and showing me the sites of history.

One afternoon, we walked into the market square at Cambridge. Tom pointed out the market cross at the center of the square and recreated the scene in which John and Charles Wesley might have ministered to the masses who gathered in the marketplace. For the most part, the market square served as the gathering point for the poor—millers and miners, hungry and homeless, beggars and thieves. Drunken brawls, gambling calls, vulgar seductions and ear-splitting curses contaminated the air. Into the middle of the masses, John and Charles came to preach the gospel. Charles led the way by climbing the three or four stone steps at the base of the market cross. Standing above the crowd he began to sing. The tune was familiar but the words were new.

> O for a thousand tongues to sing
> My great Redeemer's praise
> The glories of my God and king.
> The triumphs of His grace.

The clear, pure note of joy caught the attention of the raucous crowd. Never before had they heard a word of hope in a religious song. Brawling, gambling, begging, cursing and buying stopped. John Wesley then mounted the steps, took hold of the cross and announced God's grace—free in all and free for all. Throughout England, the Wesley brothers repeated the pattern—singing a note of joy and speaking the message of grace. Thousands upon thousands heard them and responded. The eighteenth-century Wesleyan Revival swept over the nation and saved its soul.

The "oil of joy" prepared the way for Wesley to preach the gospel. Charles Wesley wrote more than 600 hymns. In each of them, the tone is joy and the message is grace. Christian leaders will do well to remember that the same anointing with the "oil of joy" in any setting will set them apart and prepare the way for their mission. Especially in Christian organizations, joy is expected to be the tone.

My sister, Patricia McKenna Seraydarian, has written a book entitled *The Church Secretary*. After calling church offices and getting responses from secretaries that ranged from cold professionalism to giddy spirituality, she felt compelled to write a manual for church secretaries which emphasized their role as "ministry." Both personal and professional qualities contribute to the tone they set as the first voice or face which people identify with the church.

Like the entry point to a building, the "counter people" at the entry point to our organizations create lasting impressions. If the tone they set is "joy," our work is enhanced. But if the tone is cold, noncaring or gruff, not even a strong public relations department can overcome the handicap. Leaders who are responsible for setting the tone of their organization will make sure that the "oil of joy" flows to and from the entry points where people get their first impression of Christians in action.

Our Incarnate Joy

As further distinction for the role of the Christian leader, Incarnate joy is the tone within which the redemptive vision is seen and the servant mission is stated. Our study of Jesus' joy reveals these working principles:

1. "Joy" is a biblical concept that cannot be understood apart from the Incarnation of Jesus Christ.
2. Joy escapes exact definition because it is a surprising expression of natural emotion and supernatural confirmation.
3. Joy is not a goal to be stated, pursued or achieved, but a benefit of seeking Christ as our "overwhelming first."
4. Joy is a gift of the Holy Spirit who fuses the "pure joy" of being in the Presence of God with the "practical joy" of being in His service.
5. Joy is an intrinsic value which is independent of circumstances. Hence, it is sustained or even enhanced in suffering.
6. Joy, according to Jesus, is bearing the name of God, obeying the will of God, speaking the Word of God and doing the work of God.
7. Joy is contagious. If a Christian leader has the joy of Christ, it will spread to followers and pervade the organization.
8. Joy is persuasive. At the edges of our leadership and at the entry points into our organizations where "outsiders" see us first, the "oil of joy" is the best preparation for our mission.

The strategy for Incarnational leadership is now complete. It is not a plan, a ploy, a pattern or a position, but a perspective identified with the Incarnational person of Jesus Christ. Entering into His strategy, we see the vision of redemption, we state the mission of servanthood and we set the tone of joy. No other leadership strategy is quite the same. Through the work of the Holy Spirit, divine and human dimensions come together giving Christian leadership its distinction. Incarnate joy is the seal of our strategy and the reward for our servanthood.

Case in Point

A new college president inherited a climate of self-doubt among the faculty and students of the campus community. Both the history of the supporting denomination and the background of the college reinforced the pessimism. The church struggled with a small, poor, rural constituency and a self-effacing theology. The college stood in the midst of a scrubby village with a long history of debt, an in-grown faculty, and a shrinking, nonselective student body.

Visitors to the campus were greeted by a gum-chewing receptionist in slacks and T-shirt, who mumbled "Hello" and provided an escort to the Dean of Students' office. He immediately apologized for dowdy students blocking the doorway. Over a cup of coffee, he complained about babysitting students who didn't belong in college. Later, a faculty member confirmed his complaint by ruing the remedial work required while longing for vigorous intellectual exchange. Every indicator on campus pointed to a high "misery index."

In the new president's office, the scene changed. A competent and articulate bundle of energy who had been called of God to the position unveiled a vision for turning the college around.

Without creating an artificial climate of false gladness, the president wants to raise the tone and renew the spirit of the campus. He asks your advice.

1. Where would you start? With what key people would you work?

2. How does tone-setting relate to the leader's responsibilities for seeing the vision and stating the mission? Are they sequential or integral in development?

3. How can you as a leader communicate Incarnational joy without making it appear to be an end in itself?

Part Three

Our Incarnate Task

OUR INCARNATE MODEL
"BUILDING HIS TEAM"

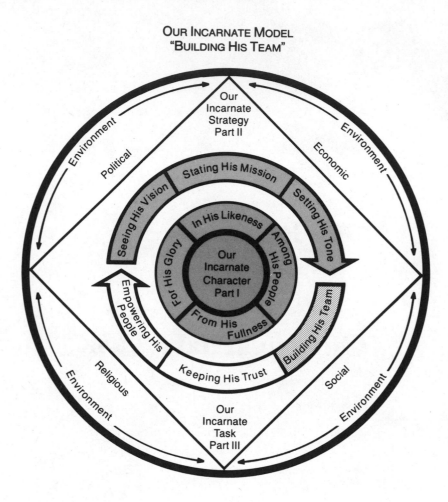

> "Come, follow Me," Jesus said,
> *"and I will make you fishers of men."*
> Mark 1:17 NIV

10

Building His Team

Strategic planning is not enough. A leader must implement the plans. The tools for implementation are managing and doing. Certainly, Jesus was a doer. He communicated His redemptive vision by preaching and teaching; He modeled His servant mission by serving the poor and needy. But His priority task for implementing His strategy was to recruit, organize and develop disciples. Incarnation continues as we see Him leading His twelve companions through the stages of (1) forming, (2) norming, (3) storming and (4) performing—a process that is familiar to any leader who has tried to build a team.

The Forming Stage

Mark, the Gospel writer, loved the word "immediately." He used it to accent the timely and significant actions of Jesus. For example, "immediately" after Jesus announced His public ministry, He went to the Sea of Galilee to begin recruiting His disciples. This was His first task, indicating the priority that

He gave to team-building. Peter Drucker put it most succinctly when he said, "A leader is a person with followers." Expanding that same idea in the context of Jesus' action, we must add, "An Incarnational leader is a person who builds disciples."

In another book, *Renewing Our Ministry,* I have outlined the raw materials for discipleship which Jesus saw in Peter, James and John when He called out to them, "Come, follow me and I will make you to become fishers of men." As unlikely and as unprepared as they were, Jesus saw them as trustworthy, teachable and task-oriented men. When He asked for their commitment to Him, He in turn made His commitment to them—to be the model for their trust, mentor for their teaching and manager of their results.[1]

Incarnate leaders make the same commitment to their followers—to be their model, mentor and manager. This commitment should be part of the evaluation of our leadership. To be sure, performance and achievement in relation to organizational goals must be scrutinized. But equally important, perhaps more important, are these counterpoints of leadership commitment:

> Am I a model for trust?
> Am I a mentor for teaching?
> Am I a manager of results?

Selecting Ordinary People

Jesus chose ordinary people for His Incarnational team. Their diversity of backgrounds, vocations and outlooks added to His team-building challenge. Either their surnames, family names or identification by vocation and temperament suggest that He selected such a heterogeneous crew that unity seemed well-nigh impossible. Certainly, they were a far cry from the conformity that lends to cohesion in team-building. IBM, for instance, credits its strength to the similarity of its people

in shared values, professional satisfactions and even unifor-
mity of dress. In general, the working principle is this: the
strongest organizational culture is sustained by people who
conform to that culture.

Jesus took a major risk with the persons He chose to be
His disciples. None of them was theologically sophisticated,
trained for leadership or primed for a public image. Yet,
strange as it seems, Jesus chose them for their independence,
diversity and nonconformity. But, in the long run, their differences could be their strengths. If they could be molded
into a team that shared His vision and extended His mission,
their diversity would make them effective in a variety of
cultures across the world. One of the tests of Incarnational
leadership is whether or not we can appreciate and develop
persons with whom we differ in personality, style and outlook. If we are extroverts, can we work with an introvert? If
our leadership style is transformational, can we encourage
the development of transactional leaders? If we are realists,
can we handle an idealist?

Jesus formed a team out of all types of people. Make no
mistake, it wasn't easy. On the night before He chose His
twelve disciples, He prayed through the night. As a person
who has always had to make staff decisions, I can enter His
thoughts during that night of prayer because I too have lain
awake thinking and praying about a staff appointment. I can
imagine Him asking such questions as these:

Who has taste and judgment?
Who has a good public reputation and practical wisdom?
Upon whom does the Spirit of the Lord rest?
Which are the quick learners?
Who can I trust?
Whose past performance predicts future success?
Who are the risk-takers?
Which have the gifts that match our mission?
After I am gone, who will continue my ministry?

No candidate met all the qualifications. Yet, like all leaders, Jesus had to make a decision—choosing some, losing others and living with the consequences. President Abraham Lincoln said of his personnel decisions, "Whenever I make an appointment out of ten candidates, I make one ingrate and nine enemies."

Until you have made personnel decisions of this nature, you don't know the lonely struggle of executive leadership. Even now, I am torn between my desire to trust the judgment of a subordinate and the intuitive sense that a pending appointment is wrong. While I have not prayed all night, my sleep has been disturbed.

As experience grows, our intuition becomes more accurate. Seasoned executives will admit that their decisions are eighty percent intuition and twenty percent reason. For this reason alone, we must not forsake the counsel of our elder statesmen.

A youth culture is one of the symptoms of our secular society. We put the elders on the shelf and suffer when the young repeat the errors of the past. A biblical viewpoint does not support either one-dimensional or one-generational leadership. When the Spirit of God falls upon human flesh, whether at Pentecost or today, the young see visions, the old dream dreams and the middle-aged prophesy. A biblical time perspective for leadership must include the dreams of the old, the visions of the young and the prophecies of the middle-aged which serve as a balance between the old and the young.

After years of experience in the presidency of Christian higher education, I frequently find myself turning a staff decision over and over again, viewing all facets, weighing all options and asking my colleagues to check another angle. What may appear to be skepticism or reluctance is the product of painful experience. My career is dotted with choices that proved to be wrong, most commonly caused by the assumption that people will change when promoted or moved. Now, I invariably invoke the principle: *past performance is the best predictor of future performance.* In this context,

I have learned to sort out the difference between character flaws and situational failures. The latter may be corrected; the former cannot.

For instance, a bright, young person overwhelmed me with charm, creativity and sparkling stories of accomplishment. Consequently, I eased up on reference checks and hired him on the spot. He advanced rapidly to a visible position of responsibility in the institution, but two years later, the flaw of falsified credentials came to light. No choice remained. I fired him without a public explanation to permit him to find other employment. The flak flew because his "Pied Piper" personality had gathered followers who heard only his intriguing tune.

Another lesson in recruiting disciples was learned. From then on, I have insisted upon spending nickels on the front edge of a staff decision rather than paying dollars later on. My only comfort from that experience is to remember that Jesus appointed Judas Iscariot as one of His disciples. Second-guessing the circumstances, I can imagine that Judas had sparkling credentials for discipleship, except for a character flaw. Whether Jesus foresaw that flaw, circumstances exposed it, God ordained it or Satan exploited it, is a matter of conjecture. More important is the recognition that the selection of staff and disciples is the make-or-break point for implementing our Incarnational strategy.

Especially in staff selection, you have to keep your sense of humor. A new vice president and I had prolonged discussions about staff appointments. He tended to promote people in order to solve their problems. So I repeatedly pressed the principle that future performance is best predicted by past performance. Then I left the decision to him. Later, when he came in with reports of continuing problems, I found myself saying, "I told you so" too many times. One day I scribbled the words, "I told you so," on one of my yellow memos and suggested that he put it in the top drawer of his desk. To assure him I vowed, "Never again will I say 'I told you so.'" The yellow memo became an unspoken code between us.

Often, when discussing a staff problem, our eyes would meet with laughter as he chuckled, "I know—the yellow memo in the top drawer."

Organizing the Team

One of the on-going debates among management experts is the question, "Which comes first, strategy or structure?" In one sense, it is a chicken-and-egg debate. But in another sense, the answer is obvious. If strategy does not determine structure, structure will decide strategy. Jesus' Incarnational vision "to seek and save the lost" cannot be dictated by structure. The most disappointing and frustrating moments in the history of the church have come when the structure— whether dictatorial rule, bureaucratic hierarchy or personality cult—has blurred the redemptive vision, diverted the servant mission or muffled the joyful tone of our Incarnational strategy.

Jesus organized His diverse group of disciples with a view toward the effective implementation and future extension of His strategic mission. Purposefully, He chose just twelve disciples whom He designated as "apostles" (Mark 3:13). The number is significant. Research in group dynamics suggests that twelve to fifteen persons constitute the "critical mass" for intensive learning and personalized interaction. Within the acknowledged limits of time for teaching, Jesus had to internalize His vision, mission and tone with a few disciples rather than many.

Next, He organized His team by levels of leadership. Within the group of twelve, Peter, James and John constituted what might be called His "executive committee." Among the three, Peter served as *primus* among peers. These disciples became His closest friends and confidants. Jesus took them with Him to witness His glory on the Mount of Transfiguration and counted upon them to sustain Him during His passion in the Garden of Gethsemane. Even then, their differences caused controversy. Peter was hot-tempered, James and

John were "sons of thunder"—ambitious and argumentative. In contemporary terms, they were "bull-headed" bundles of energy, and yet as tender as tabby cats. Peter wilted before the joshing of a chamber maid, James was a "Momma's boy" and John became the substitute son whom Jesus gave the responsibility to care for His mother.

Only in perspective do we see why Jesus chose them. Once empowered by the Holy Spirit, these tough minds and tender hearts became ready expressions of Christ's Incarnational traits, "full of grace and truth." Until that time, however, Jesus had to be directive in His leadership with them. So directive, in fact, that He commanded Peter, "Out of my sight, Satan" (Mark 8:33 NIV).

As the third step in organizing His team, Jesus paired the disciples for mutual support and action. Although the initial appointment makes no distinction among the disciples except for Peter, James and John, Jesus soon recognized the need to avoid the problems of "isolates" and "loners." By teaming the disciples two by two (or what is called "dyads" in organizational structure), He set up a "peer review" system for both support and evaluation.

Every leader needs a confidant with whom to share the highs and lows of Incarnational action. The glow of success can quickly lead to self-glory and the impact of failure can activate defensive self-deprecation. Either can be fatal for the Incarnate leader. So, Jesus extended their support and accountability system from Himself into teams of two. Because of the interactive learning between the disciple partners, Jesus could be more coach than commander.

The more we learn about Christian leadership, the more we appreciate the organizational genius of Jesus. Only as we create a multifaceted matrix of support and accountability around our leaders will we restore the personal trustworthiness, credibility, public confidence and professional competence required for the complex and changing times ahead. Jesus' Incarnational structure gives us a pattern. Even with the transforming power of the Holy Spirit in their lives, His disciples needed a human system of check and balance to avoid the extremes of human or spiritual temptation.

Once Jesus had established the core of His organization in the twelve disciples, He extended His leadership in a network of seventy-two others, two by two (Luke 10:1). A model of networking opens before us. The twelve disciples who were divided into teams of two for their first preaching, teaching and healing venture, were now given the delegated responsibility to lead twelve others into the field. Jesus gave His first disciples little time to bask in their accomplishments. The acid test of Incarnational leadership is the ability to communicate the redemptive vision, implement the servant mission and sound the note of joy with others.

The pattern for world evangelization was also set. From the Incarnate Christ, the teams of two and the groups of twelve, an ever-expanding, exponential network was envisioned that would embrace the world. Structure revealed Jesus' strategy for Incarnational leadership: every Christian becomes a follower and leader at the same time.

The Norming Stage

In the process of team-building, "norming" follows "forming" and never stops. Basically, the leader is responsible for setting the level of expectations for his or her followers. Three criteria apply. The expectations must be (1) high, (2) clear and (3) consistent. High, but attainable, expectations motivate rather than discourage people; clear and specific expectations mean that people know exactly what is expected of them so that they can proceed without surprises. Then, to complete the criteria, expectations must be consistent with the strategy of the organization and with each other. Inconsistency at either point results in frustration and demoralization that undermines effectiveness.

Leaders establish norms for their followers both generally and specifically. Through His preaching and teaching, Jesus communicated His redemptive vision and enunciated the principles of the kingdom of God. His Sermon on the Mount, for instance, is a general statement of the norms for kingdom values and conduct. The parables are more specific in teaching a single truth through symbols. Private sessions with the disciples were taken to explain and apply the truth of the parables. Whatever His method of communication, Jesus never let up on the process of building and reinforcing the norms of the kingdom.

Using Mundane Tools

Effective leaders are masters of symbols. Just as Jesus utilized the common symbols of nature, experience and history in His communication as a leader, contemporary studies of leadership are rediscovering symbol-making as a skill and tool of management.[2] Top leaders use symbols to communicate and reinforce their vision, mission and tone in vivid and varied ways.

Eloquence in communicating verbal symbols is a gift that we usually associate with effective leaders. Certainly, the gift cannot be denied. But verbal eloquence is less effective than the use of the mundane tools of time, space and modeling that are available to every leader. The way a leader spends *time,* for example, is watched by every follower because the use of time is a symbol of priorities.

For instance, Jesus seems to have spent most of His time alone with His disciples. While the Scriptural text records His sermons to the masses, debates with the Pharisees and interactions with individuals, the Gospel account is interspersed with the priority time that He gave to His disciples, explaining His sayings, evaluating their performance and getting their feedback.

Followers are also ardent watchers of the amount of time that leaders give to their role. To the surprise of those who thought that successful leaders lolled in the luxury of time, facts show that they work harder and longer than their subordinates. Whereas we used to have the "leisure classes and the working masses," we now have the "working classes and the leisure masses"—a new challenge indeed.

Space is also a mundane tool that a leader may use as a symbol to reinforce vision and mission. In accordance with His vision "to seek and to save the lost," Jesus went from town to town and into the fields to preach, teach and heal. In their book *Leaders,* Bennis and Nanus tell of a chief executive officer who simply unlocked the front door and invited employees to come in the front rather than the back as a symbol that people had priority in the new administration.[3]

Symbols of time and space, however, are secondary to the *modeling* of mission by which Jesus set the norms for His disciples. In the old dilemma of managing versus doing, Jesus chose hands-on doing over arms'-length managing. But even His "doing" served as a means of managing. His choice sets the standard for us. If we get too far away from the trenches where mission meets need and program meets people, we not only lose touch with our followers, but we also forfeit the value of modeling as a mundane tool for setting the norms of expectations for our followers.

Peter Drucker believes that the best way to avoid the corrupting influences of power, sex and wealth which have plagued Christian leadership is to set periods of time for performing at the point where mission meets need and program serves people. Role modeling, psychiatrists say, may be the most important discovery of the past decade in determining the effectiveness of leadership. In confirmation of their observation, research studies have shown that preaching leaders produce preaching followers. Only when preaching and practice are consistently combined in the modeling of the leader will the result be preaching and practicing disciples.[4]

Defining the Task

The mundane tools of time, space and role-modeling are generalized examples of norming in the team-building process. The task description for the person is the more specific

statement of expectations upon which progress and performance can be monitored. Criteria for a task description
include:

1. Title.
2. Line of authority.
3. Line of responsibility.
4. Relationship of role to mission.
5. Description of task expectation in qualitative and,
   wherever possible, measurable terms.
6. Professional qualifications required for the role and
   tasks.
7. Personal qualifications for the role.
8. Compensation and terms of agreement.

Jesus must have had similar criteria in mind when He appointed His twelve disciples. Their task description included:

1. *Title*—apostles.
2. *Authority*—to cast out demons.
3. *Responsibility*—to Him.
4. *Task*—to preach the good news and heal the sick.

Significantly, Jesus also included a highly personalized
qualification in His task description for the disciples. He
wanted them "to be with Him." Companionship and friendship are seldom stated in task descriptions. In fact, we think
the opposite. As former President Richard Nixon said the
other day, "Presidents and vice-presidents don't have to like
each other. If they win the election, they'll be bosom bud-
dies." But in Christian leadership, the need of companions
and friendship cannot be denied.

Leadership is a lonely position. Like Simeon the Stylite, a
leader often feels as if he or she is perched high on a pedestal
and all alone in the burning sun. Jesus knew that He would
eventually alienate Jewish leaders, be rejected by His home-
folk, disappoint the fickle masses and be deserted by His

disciples. As His circle of support grew smaller and smaller, He needed more than disciples who shared His redemptive vision and extended His servant mission. Jesus needed friends to encourage and counsel Him. When He included companionship in the task description for the apostles, we can never doubt His full identification with human leaders and His full appreciation for our loneliness.

Just as Jesus chose ordinary people as His disciples, He used mundane tools to establish the norms for their task. While we are tempted to communicate our vision by inspired oratory and gracious gestures, Jesus used the mundane tools of time and space to communicate His redemptive vision and model His servant mission.

The Storming Stage

Conflict is inevitable in a context of change. Especially in the development of diverse and dissimilar disciples, interpersonal conflict is part and parcel of the nurturing and norming process. The very diversity of Jesus' disciples increased their volatility. We should not be surprised, then, when we read about conflict between them. Three kinds of conflict are revealed in the Gospel of Mark: (1) public conflict over the failure of the disciples to heal the epileptic boy; (2) interpersonal conflict over who would be greatest in the kingdom of heaven; and (3) intergroup conflict over the authority for ministry.

Jesus showed patience in each case. He began with a diagnosis of the root cause and proceeded to resolve the conflict by bringing the disciples to common ground and then lifting their sights to a higher, common cause. For the interpersonal conflicts over who would be greatest in the kingdom of heaven, Jesus did not rebuke their ambition. Instead, He linked greatness with servanthood, thus reinforcing His mission once again in the minds of the apostles. Then, taking a child into His arms as a symbol of the "poor" whom He came to serve, Jesus said:

> Whoever welcomes one of these little children in my name welcomes me; and whoever welcomes me does not welcome me but the one who sent me.
>
> Mark 9:37 NIV

What started out as a conflict over status was resolved on the common ground of servanthood with the symbol of a child as a reminder that the highest priority of Incarnational strategy is given to "the last, the least, and the lost" among them.

Jesus handled the intergroup conflict in the same way. Representing the disciples, John told Him:

> Teacher . . . we saw a man driving out demons in your name and we told him to stop, because he was not one of us.
>
> Mark 9:38 NIV

Finding common ground in those who bear His name and do His work, Jesus resolved the conflict by saying:

> Do not stop him. . . . No one who does a miracle in my name can in the next moment say anything bad about me, for whoever is not against us is for us.
>
> Mark 9:39–40 NIV

Still, the dispute did not go away. "Storming" appears over and over again in the development of disciples. Especially if the root is in human nature, such as the drive for status or power, leaders can count upon its repetition. My experience suggests that power is always a latent and lingering source of conflict which can surface again and again. To describe the situation, I have said, "The hatchet may be buried, but the handle is close to the surface."

In their book *Leadership and Ambiguity,* March and Cohen identify certain institutions, such as universities and hospitals, as "organized anarchies." Vividly and realistically, they see the perennial issues which stalk leaders as leftovers in a garbage can. When you try to get to the bottom of the problem and take hold of the issue, it comes out over and over again with a lot of messy and smelly stringers.[5]

Not more than a day or two after Jesus resolved the status conflict between James and John, the issue surfaced again. They requested the privilege of sitting at Jesus' right and left hand when He established His kingdom. The other ten disciples were livid, probably to the point of verbal violence and physical expulsion for the "Sons of Thunder." Alert to the crisis, Jesus intervened immediately. Taking the glowering group aside, Jesus exercised His genius in conflict resolution by again bringing the disciples to common ground. They all despised the Gentiles and their penchant for power and glory as seen daily in the brutality and pomp of the Romans. Without singling out James and John by name or saying that all of the disciples had the same ambition, Jesus let them know how corrupting the lust for power can be.

Thus, the stage was set for turning a critical conflict into a meaningful resolution. Jesus repeated the call to the mission of servanthood and used Himself, the Son of Man whose power and position are supreme, as the model:

> For even the Son of Man did not come to be served, but to serve, and to give His life as a ransom for many.
>
> Mark 10:45

A pattern for conflict resolution among "storming" disciples is thus established. First, Jesus accepted conflict as another opportunity for developing His disciples. Second, He confronted the conflicting parties immediately. Third, He diagnosed the root of the problem in human nature. Fourth, He moved the conflict to common ground where the protagonists agreed. Fifth, He found a common symbol with which the parties could affirmatively identify. Sixth, He used the occasion to refocus His vision and reinforce His mission in the minds of His "storming" disciples. Seventh and finally, He patiently and positively dealt with conflict even when the problem surfaced repeatedly in different guises.

Incarnational leaders will exercise these same principles with "storming" members of their team.

The Performing Stage

Performing, quantitatively and qualitatively, is the leader's goal in developing the Incarnational team. Although Jesus' disciples are best remembered for their miraculous acts after Jesus returned to His Father, we may forget that they were prepared to perform while under the tutelage of Jesus.

Our current pattern of education tends to divide preparation and performance into separate and sequential periods of time. Robert Hutchins, the "boy wonder" president of the University of Chicago, described college as a four-year period during which the young are kept out of trouble until they can get a job.

Not so for Jesus' students. Very soon after their appointment as apostles and before they could possibly absorb the full meaning of Jesus' redemptive vision or enact the methods of His servant mission, they were sent into the field two by two. Their task description as apostles is now filled out with these instructions:

> Take nothing for the journey except a staff—no bread, no bag, no money in your belts. Wear sandals but not an extra tunic. Whenever you enter a house, stay there until you leave that town. And if any place will not welcome you or listen to you, shake the dust off your feet when you leave, as a testimony against them.
>
> Mark 6:8–11 NIV

The expectations for their apostleship are high, clear and consistent. They are to depend exclusively upon God for their livelihood. Even an extra tunic might be a barrier to their identification with the poor. They are to avoid being spoiled by competing households, and in the economy of time and space, they are to keep moving. Readiness for the gospel is a condition for their strategy. If people do not welcome them or listen to them, they are to make the dramatic gesture of shaking the dust off their feet as a sign of rejection. All these instructions point to another salient fact. Incarnate leaders cannot become "apostles-in-place." They must keep moving on.

Jesus' instructions remind me of a saying among missionaries, "You can tell their commitment by the way they pack their bags." Missionaries who give themselves incarnationally to live among the people of another culture will be sensitive to the symbols of dress and demeanor which signify either identification or separation. So it was with the disciples. As further symbolic representation of Jesus' vision "to seek and to save the lost," by focusing upon the poor, the disciples were to pack their bags incarnationally by living among the people and identifying with them.

There is another reason, however, for Jesus' instructions to the disciples. In an Incarnational paradox, He wants them to be independent of people at the same time that He wants the disciples to identify with them. The gospel requires a degree of objectivity to be effective. Leaders often learn this lesson the hard way. With the need for friendship, there is the risk of favoritism. On the first day after my appointment as a college president, I met a long-term friend on the street who also served as a faculty member. As in the past, I talked rather freely about my perceptions after one day in the office. To my surprise, the words came back to me the next day as an official pronouncement.

In our second presidency, my wife and I became part of a small group of faculty members who thoroughly enjoyed each other's company in social settings. One of the rules of our informal association was to avoid talking shop when we were together. Yet, when budget time came and I had to make decisions between programs, I heard the accusation of favoritism for one of my friends. The truth of the matter was that the administrator-friend in question did a superior job of preparing the budget request and justifying the program, but that became incidental.

With great regret, we had to pull away from the group as one of the costs of leadership. The experience helps me understand the independence that Jesus required for His disciples. Tension between identification with people and the independence from people is inevitable. Unless the Holy Spirit keeps us constantly in balance, we will veer to one side or the other.

Effective performance resulted when the disciples followed Jesus' instructions. Mark reports:

> They went out and preached that people should repent. They drove out many demons and anointed many sick people with oil and healed them.
>
> Mark 6:12–13 NIV

With the authority to preach, the power to cast out demons and the example of Jesus' healing, they justified His confidence in them. On their second mission venture, when Jesus added the responsibility for leading twelve others, the seventy-two returned with a shout of joy, "Lord, even the demons submit to us in your name" (Luke 10:17 NIV). Note the confirmation of joy. By obeying the will of God, speaking the Word of God, invoking the Name of God and doing the work of God, they saw joy crown their work and confirm their results.

Celebrating Small Wins

Hidden in these verses is the basic leadership principle for performance. Jesus utilized the "theory of small wins" long before Tom Peters, co-author of the book, *In Search of Excellence,* coined the phrase.[6] The vision to seek and to save the lost can be overwhelming to ordinary people and the strategy of servanthood can be discouraging to students who are still learning skills. But by focusing the vision upon a small segment of people and "chunking" the mission into manageable pieces, Jesus showed us how to get results and gain satisfaction. Though the disciples' "wins" from their field trips may have been "small" in comparison with the task ahead, they returned to Jesus with ecstatic reports. Incarnational leaders always take into account human limits as well as divine possibilities.

As part of the responsibility for developing His disciples, Jesus monitored the results of their performance. His feedback to them came immediately after they returned, whether reporting success or failure. When they returned with the jubilant report that even demons obeyed them, Jesus responded with a glimpse into His eternal power and glory as the Son of God, but followed with the caution against abusing the power that He had given them. Then, in another of those private moments when Jesus shared privileged information with His disciples, He added the insight:

> Blessed are the eyes that see what you see. For I tell you that many prophets and kings wanted to see what you see but did not see it, and to hear what you hear but did not hear it.
> Luke 10:23–24 NIV

The reward for their performance is the privilege of seeing the veil of God's revelation lifted and hearing the Word of God from the lips of His Son.

Jesus' responsibility for monitoring the performance of the disciples involves dealing with their failures as well as their successes. In their interviews with top leaders, Bennis and Nanus found that they do not think about "winning or losing" but about "winning or learning." As one executive said, "It's like skiing. If you're not falling down, you're not learning."[7] For them, every failure becomes a learning experience. Jesus had this same attitude. When He came down from the Mount of Transfiguration all aglow with the glory of God, He met defeated disciples, a frustrated mob and disputing teachers of the law. Try as they might, His disciples had failed to heal an epileptic boy. Jesus' first reaction is understandable. After all of His patient teaching, modeling and interning for His disciples, they had lapsed into powerless dodos. "O unbelieving generation," Jesus scolded them, "how long shall I stay with you?" (Mark 9:19 NIV).

Because patience is not one of my virtues, I like Jesus'

response. I also like the idea that He took things into His own hands and healed the boy. I, too, would rather do it myself because I believe I can do it faster and better than my slow-learning colleagues. But when I do take over, I miss the opportunity for teaching that Jesus found when His disciples asked Him behind closed doors, "Why couldn't we drive it out?" The Lord answered, "This kind comes out only by prayer." From their failure, the disciples learned one of the most fundamental lessons of their lives. The depth of our spiritual resources determines the kind of demons we can conquer.

Our Incarnational task of team-building is ever before us. The full and continuing process is outlined in Figure 6.

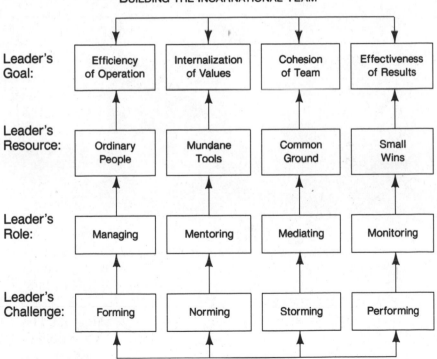

BUILDING THE INCARNATIONAL TEAM

Leader's Goal:	Efficiency of Operation	Internalization of Values	Cohesion of Team	Effectiveness of Results
Leader's Resource:	Ordinary People	Mundane Tools	Common Ground	Small Wins
Leader's Role:	Managing	Mentoring	Mediating	Monitoring
Leader's Challenge:	Forming	Norming	Storming	Performing

Figure 6

142   OUR INCARNATE TASK

As Incarnate leaders, we are called to be *managers* with the responsibility for recruiting and organizing ordinary people into an expanding and efficient network which will embrace the whole world. As *mentors,* we must communicate the redemptive vision of Jesus Christ through familiar symbols and with mundane tools while modeling our strategy for servanthood through our doing. Along the way there will be conflicts with which we must deal in a timely, patient and creative manner. As *mediators,* our task is to find common ground among protagonists so that the conflicts can be turned into opportunities for reinforcing our vision and our mission. Our goal, then, is to serve as *monitors* evaluating the effective performance and celebrating the small wins of our followers who, in turn, become leaders of others. In them and in us, the note of joy will sound as our reward. This is Incarnational leadership at its best.

Case in Point

Leadership style has been likened to a musical performance. Some leaders are best as *soloists*—self-directed and totally responsible for their own performance. Other leaders are like conductors of a *symphonic orchestra*—delegating the playing to a variety of instrumentalists who follow the same score under the conductor's direction. Still other leaders perform best in a *jazz group*—giving the downbeat and participating personally in a small group of independent players who improvise on a common theme.

1. As a leader, which style do you prefer?

2. Which style best represents the organization of which you are a part? Is there another musical analogy that better fits your organization? If your preference differs from your organization, how do you reconcile the two?

3. Does a leader's style vary from time to time—soloist, orchestra conductor or jazz player?

4. Which style best represents the leadership of Jesus with His disciples?

5. Christian leadership throughout history varies all the way from infallible popes to desert monks and from denominational superchurches to parachurch movements. Is there a preferred style for the church or does God use all types to achieve His purpose? Which is most effective?

6. As a Christian leader responsible for team-building, what is the current stage of your efforts—norming, forming, storming or performing? Does the cycle ever end? Is storming normal or abortive to the process? How do you resolve conflicts in the storming stage?

OUR INCARNATE MODEL
"KEEPING HIS TRUST"

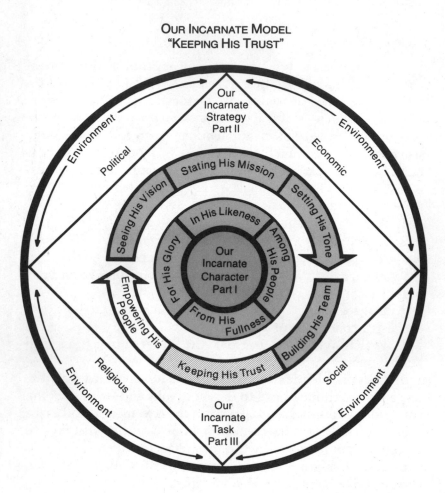

Now my heart is troubled, and what shall I say? Father, save me from this hour? No, it was for this very reason that I came to this hour. Father, glorify your name.

John 12:27–28 NIV

11

Keeping His Trust

Leaders who manage and monitor others must first manage and monitor themselves. The responsibility increases for those of us who are called to be Incarnational Christian leaders. Our stewardship and servanthood will be called into accountability before God, not just on judgment day, but every day, and especially in those moments when our leadership is put on the line by personal temptations and pivotal decisions. Management literature identifies these types of turning points as "critical incidents" when our decisions make the difference between effective and ineffective leadership. The stakes increase for Incarnational Christian leaders when our spirituality as well as our strategy is put on the line.

Defining the Critical Incident

Most of the time a leader's task is routine. The functions of planning, staffing, organizing, directing, coordinating, reporting and budgeting are familiar to anyone with

145

management responsibilities, Christian or secular. For the most part these skills can be learned by schooling and experience. When I think about my role as a college, university and seminary president, for instance, I realize that many people could do most of my work. But then I remember the "critical incidents" in my career which determined whether I was an effective or ineffective leader. My critical incidents include decisions on purpose and policy recommendations for institutions, moral and spiritual problems with people, economic and educational proposals on programs, interpersonal conflicts and personal career choices. In each case, my leadership was on the line and my decisions had long-range, even eternal, consequences. Let me give an example that may seem more temporal than eternal, but at the time of its happening, it was just as "critical" for either realm.

In 1976, I made the recommendation that Seattle Pacific College be renamed "Seattle Pacific University." Preceding the recommendation were faculty studies, market research, comparable cases and opinion surveys of campus, community, alumni and church constituencies. When all the available data were in, I reviewed the options and found that any recommendation required a risk. As Winston Churchill noted, leadership must always operate when "the proportions are veiled in mist." So, after weighing all the factors, I put my leadership on the line with the recommendation to change the name from "college" to "university." My reservations had to be put aside as I had to defend the recommendation against opposition. Finally, the call for a vote resulted in the two-thirds majority required for the change. My private "second thoughts" during a sleepless night faded when the morning paper carried the headline announcing the change. We had crossed the Rubicon; there was no turning back.

Although a "critical incident" such as this may seem to be too subjective a measure for leadership effectiveness, the technique is touted by management experts as one of the best of their instruments.

Flanagan fathered the idea of the "critical incident" as a

prime indicator of a manager's effectiveness.[1] Typically we measure a manager's effectiveness in quantitative terms, such as the amount of production and the margin of profitability. A "critical incident" is far more subjective, but no less important. Critical incidents are often identified through stories and anecdotes, not unlike the mundane tools for team-building. When brought into cluster by factor analysis, they become a valuable measure for the effectiveness of leadership.

Flanagan described a "critical incident" by four criteria: (1) the situation and the circumstances that lead to it; (2) the person's decision; (3) the consequences that followed; and (4) whether or not the person had control over the situation. By identifying the cluster of critical incidents that are part of any given job, then, Falkenberg and others found that this technique was one of the best for distinguishing between effective and ineffective performance.

Presidents of our nation provide the most dramatic examples of "critical incidents" by which their leadership is assessed. Roosevelt had his Yalta; Truman his Hiroshima; Eisenhower his Korean War; Kennedy his Cuba; Johnson his Vietnam; Nixon his Watergate; Carter his hostages; and Reagan his Contras. Although most of these decisions involve foreign policy, similar decisions on the domestic scene could be gathered as part of the cluster of critical incidents that make or break the effectiveness of our presidents.

Not all critical incidents are of such magnitude. Our oldest son, Douglas, a Professor of Organization and Management at Seattle Pacific University, designed an instrument to measure the effectiveness of faculty advisors in higher education based upon the way they handled "critical incidents" in their role with students. After identifying the multiple functions they performed as advisors, he used factor analysis to determine which of those functions were "critical." In the cluster of critical incidents, one function stood out. The most critical factor in determining effectiveness was whether or not the advisor said, "Hello," and called the student by name when they met on the campus. What appeared to be a mundane situation turned out to be a critical incident.

Building upon Flanagan's concept and extending its meaning into the context of Incarnational leadership, we see that four factors set the conditions for a "critical incident:"

1. *Circumstances:* What led up to the critical incident and why was the incident critical to the leader?
2. *Conflict:* What are the choices in tension which caused the leader to struggle with the decision?
3. *Choice:* What choice was made and why?
4. *Consequences:* What were the results of the choice for the effectiveness or ineffectiveness of the leader?

The consequences of the leader's decision in dealing with a critical incident are all-important. In their book, *Leaders,* Bennis and Nanus found four strategies of effective leaders based upon their interviews with ninety corporate executives who are considered top leaders in America.[2] The four strategies are:

1. Attention through vision,
2. Meaning through communication,
3. Trust through positioning and
4. Empowerment through self-deployment.

In each case, the leader has a responsibility and the followers have a response. A leader with a clear and focused vision will capture the attention and the commitment of followers. To be able to communicate that vision through teaching symbols and personal modeling will give meaning to the life and work of those who follow. Positioning, then, is the strategy by which a leader holds course and consistency so that followers will sense the trust in leadership that they need. Finally, by the deployment of self in time and energy, the leader empowers others to give themselves to the vision, the strategy and the task at hand. A critical incident puts each of these strategies to a decisive test.

A Critical Incident for Jesus

The passion of Jesus is introduced to us in the twelfth chapter of the Gospel of John by a "critical incident." The event is so pivotal to understanding Incarnational leadership that it warrants thorough study and personal application.

Circumstances: Immediately after the triumphal entry into Jerusalem, Greeks came to Jesus' disciples and requested an audience with Him. The request rippled up through the ranks with mounting enthusiasm. In the minds of His disciples, Jesus had come to His shining hour. The acclaim of the masses had attracted the attention of Greeks, the intellectual and cultural elite of the earth!

An unexpected dilemma unsettled Jesus. He had articulated His vision "to seek and to save the lost" and modeled His strategy as a servant to the poor. To this point in time, He had held His course against bitter opposition of Jewish leaders. Satan, however, can cause more trouble as a cooing dove than he can as a roaring lion. Cooing through the request of the Greeks, he caused Jesus more trouble than all His disputes with the Pharisees. On the surface, at least, the Greeks were innocent. They just wanted to meet Him, talk with Him and perhaps even learn from Him.

Never let it be said that Jesus was not tempted to receive the Greeks. As a Jewish carpenter's son of dubious parentage from a despised town in Galilee, He could receive no greater worldly honor. He had the chance to share His ideas with the best minds in the world, perhaps establish His own school of thought and win a niche in the Athenian Pantheon. In the best and brightest of human terms, Jesus would receive a fitting return on the glory of which He emptied Himself in order to be born a man. His response lets us know that the temptation was real, aimed at Jesus' point of vulnerability and loaded with surprise.

Conflict: When informed of the Greeks' request, Jesus begins talking to Himself. Knowing that the timing for the temptation coincides with His hour of passion, He says, "The hour has come for the Son of Man to be glorified." But which glory will He choose? The glory of the Greek or the glory of God? In answer to this inferred question, Jesus recalls His own words. They come back to haunt Him:

The Parable of the Sower:

> I tell you the truth, unless a kernel of wheat falls to the ground and dies, it remains only a single seed. But if it dies, it produces many seeds.
>
> John 12:24 NIV

The Paradox of Self-Sacrifice:

> The man who loves his life will lose it, while the man who hates his life in this world will keep it for eternal life.
>
> John 12:25 NIV

The Promise for Servanthood:

> Whoever serves me must follow me; and where I am, my servant will also be. My Father will honor the one who serves me.
>
> John 12:26 NIV

In other words, Jesus' redemptive vision, servant strategy and note of joy are in the balance. Did He really mean what He said? Would He practice what He preached? If we romanticize the Incarnation and tip the scales toward His deity, the answer seems obvious. Categorically and without hesitation, Jesus would resist the temptation and reject the Greeks.

Why then does Jesus speak of turmoil at the center of His soul?

> Now is my soul troubled, and what shall I say? Father, save me from this hour?
>
> John 12:27 NIV

He is genuinely tempted by a win–lose choice. On one side of the scales is the opportunity to live, continue to serve people and receive instant recognition as a shaper of human thought. On the other side is inevitable death, public shame and the deferred, perhaps uncertain, honor of God. The self-confession of a troubled soul tells us that Jesus gave the alternative of the Greeks serious thought. Not only His life but our redemption hung in the balance. A critical incident indeed!

Choice: Momentarily or longer, the scales teetered in the balance. Then, the weight of evidence came down heavy on the side of holding His course and rejecting the request of the Greeks. After a soul-shaking struggle, He made a momentous decision that literally moved heaven and earth. In answer to His question, "What shall I say? Father, save Me from this hour?" Jesus cast the die: "No, it was for this very reason I came to this hour. Father, glorify your name" (John 12:27–28 NIV).

God the Father instantly confirms His Son's decision, "I have glorified it, and will glorify it again" (John 12:28 NIV). As plain as those words are, the crowd did not decipher the communication between Father and Son. Some thought it thundered; others thought that an angel had spoken to Him (John 12:29).

Turning to the crowd, Jesus no longer speaks like a man in turmoil: "This voice was for your benefit, not mine" (John 12:30 NIV).

His decision is so firm that he no longer needs confirmation. Bolder yet, He throws down the gauntlet and prophesies Satan's defeat: "Now is the time for judgment on this world; now the prince of this world will be driven out" (John 12:31 NIV).

As for Himself, He prophesies with complete confidence the fulfillment of His redemptive vision and the fulfillment of His servant mission: "But I, when I am lifted up from the earth, will draw all men to myself" (John 12:32 NIV).

Despite the cadences of a death squad which are heard in the background, you can also hear a trumpet fanfare announcing the salvation of all humankind.

Consequences: The strategy for Jesus' leadership is back in focus. His vision "to seek and to save the lost" will dramatically engage the attention of all people for all time to come, not just the Greeks in their post-Golden era. No doubt remains about the meaning of His mission. He has communicated the message with the eloquence of a tumultuous personal decision. And because He has held His course and reaffirmed His position, he has earned the absolute trust of all believers. Most of all, Jesus has empowered others to see His redemptive vision and follow His servant strategy because He sacrificed His own glory for the glory of God. From the testing of His "critical incident" He emerges with His Incarnate leadership established firmly and forever.

Our Incarnate Test

From the "critical incident" which became a turning point for Jesus' leadership, we see a similar pattern in the incidents that become our Incarnate test.

1. *The circumstances arise in an Incarnational context.* Critical incidents are not isolated events without a historical background or an environmental setting. Jesus' life history as a poor boy from a despised village had a bearing upon the nature of the temptation when the Greeks requested an audience with Him. Certainly, the environmental setting of the triumphal entry which immediately preceded the Greeks' request helped pave the way for the temptation to greater glory. The historical background and environmental setting are predisposing factors which led to the critical incident. Yet, at the same time Jesus is caught by surprise. The request of the Greeks is the precipitating factor which triggers instinctive action on Jesus' part.

Several years ago, I took a sabbatical after serving seven years as a university president. The person whom I designated as chief executive in my absence had my complete confidence. He had participated in my President's Cabinet for several years and knew my mind. But six weeks into the sabbatical, he encountered a crisis on campus that created a public furor when the complainant took his case to the local press for "trial by newspaper." One phone call canceled my sabbatical. I returned home to handle the crisis. Later, a consultant reminded me that I had prepared my back-up administrator for managing in the calm, but not in crisis. Since that time, I have tried to introduce "crisis management" into my executive teaching.

2. *The conflict tests our Incarnational character.* We sometimes think that Jesus' temptation in the Wilderness became an end-all for the attempts of Satan to impugn His character and divert His mission. To the contrary, Satan returned to test Jesus repeatedly as he probed for His point of vulnerability. Satan almost found that point when he caught Jesus by surprise with the flattering request of the Greeks. Earlier, Jesus had to flee from the temptation to exchange His servant role for the crown of a king. The flight was necessary even though the struggle seemed brief. Jesus knew that mobs were fickle. They will kill you as quickly as they will make you king.

The Greeks were far less fickle. They provided the once-in-a-lifetime opportunity for Jesus to prove His self-worth and gain the glory that He had given up in the incarnation. His natural need for recognition became the tender spot for a "critical incident." It soon expanded into a test of whether or not Jesus would give up being a servant obedient to death, even death on a cross, in order to live and receive worldly honor.

All significant decisions are trade-offs. We should be suspicious of anyone who never has any live options from which to choose, no reservations to resolve and no conflict of soul in decision-making. A "critical incident," in particular, will introduce some dimensions of choice that are outside the range of our past experience or that defy the rational process for decision-making upon which we have counted in the past. Rather, we are driven back to ground-zero on our values and commitment. A "critical incident" is an Incarnational test which forces us to answer the baseline questions once again, "Will we live in His likeness, among His people, from His fullness and for His glory?"

In the Incarnational experience, our human drives for self-preservation, self-esteem and self-worth all come under test. By taking up our cross and dying with Christ, we put obedience to His will ahead of our own natural drives and desires. Then, with "Christ in us" we take the form of a servant, giving up all claim to self-interest in order to serve others. Servanthood, in Jesus' name, will bring results—often miraculous ones. But with "Christ in us," we will give up all self-glory in our own achievements. The joy of obeying God's will, speaking His Word, bearing His name and doing His work is sufficient reward. The glory is God's, the joy is ours.

One of our natural drives—self-preservation, self-esteem or self-worth—will provide an entry point for a "critical incident." As the test develops, then, our other drives will be involved. Critical incidents are like onions. The layers peel off one at a time until we come to the core. What may start out as a minor issue of self-preservation, such as turning stones into bread, can become a spiritual struggle of life-and-death proportions.

At the present time, I am thinking about a moral issue involving a colleague. Information came to me privately and anonymously. Usually, I will not respond to anonymous letters and phone calls, but in this case the evidence was incontrovertible. Suspicions without solid evidence began to circulate in the community and a small group "waited" on me with the veiled threat of revelation unless decisive executive action was taken.

Several scenarios ran through my mind. I could follow established procedure, take administrative action and receive strong support, internally and externally. But I could not escape the image of the individual in my mind. I saw a reputation ruined and an innocent family devastated. Suddenly, a fundamental question came into focus. At the risk of criticism, would I be willing to seek a solution on a personal and private basis? Even more fundamentally, would I risk my position and power for the uncertain possibility of seeing a person redeemed and a family saved?

Sometimes there is no alternative to what I call a "clean, surgical cut" which can be redeeming in its own right. In this case, however, I chose the messy route which required personal confrontation, hours of time and a long-term plan with periodic checks on progress. I failed. After two years the problem surfaced again, the wife blamed me for not involving her in the beginning and more decisive action was required. Yet, looking back, I would follow the same course. Even though I failed, the "critical incident" confirmed my commitment to err on the side of the redemptive process whenever possible.

3. *The choice tests our Incarnational strategy.* An occupational hazard of leadership is to have your words and actions thrown back in your face. Newspapers have "morgue files" which can resurrect issues from the past. Television studios have a library of videotapes which can bring scarecrows to life. In recent years, presidential candidates especially have learned that one's public life is an open book and one's private life, fair game. Presidential candidates are not alone. Every leader has to live with the words and actions of the past. A faculty member, for instance, appeared at every occasion when I spoke on the campus and furiously took notes. Curiosity led me to ask why. The answer came back that he was writing a history of the institution. I took him at his word until he pulled out his text one day to quote a statement that I had made three years earlier and raised a question about the consistency of my position. Then and there, I decided he was building a case, not writing a history.

As with Jesus, the meaning of our words comes under fire in a critical incident. Eloquence no longer counts. The question now is how we will manage ourselves as well as lead others. There is always the danger that in saving others, we ourselves become castaways. Just as in Jesus' case, the clarity of our vision, the quality of our communication, the consistency of our positioning and the sacrificial deployment of our lives are put to the test.

4. *The consequences affect the future of our Incarnational leadership.* As noted earlier, leaders have a personal responsibility for a vision that captures attention, communication that conveys meaning, positioning that earns trust and self-deployment that empowers their followers. This is why Jesus told the crowd who had heard the voice of God as the sound of thunder, or an angel speaking, "This voice was for your benefit, not mine." Once His decision had been made, His followers received the benefit. Incarnational leaders live by the principle that their purpose is not to save themselves, but to develop disciples. The Incarnate test begins with the leader—circumstances that surprise, a conflict that troubles and a choice that decides; but the consequences belong to the followers—greater attention to the redemptive vision, greater meaning for the gospel, greater trust for the position and greater sacrifice for the mission.

A word of caution about critical incidents. They are part and parcel of a leader's existence. To resolve one does not guarantee the resolution of the next one. Whether they are occupational hazards of a leader's role, accidents of history, circumstances of the environment or instruments of Satan, they return again and again in many guises.

Keep in mind that Jesus passed the Incarnate test with the Greeks only to confront the most "critical" incident of His life within a matter of minutes or hours. As He entered the Garden of Gethsemane, the test would be more than His own words returning to haunt Him. Now He had to decide whether or not to hold His course at the cost of His life. Now His redemptive vision, His servant mission and His joyful tone would be tested by a Jewish betrayal and a Roman crucifixion.

While our "critical incidents" may not be life-and-death matters, they are always tests of our effectiveness and often trials of our character. To hold our trust in such critical moments is to embody Christ and empower our followers.

Case in Point

A multinational bank opened the search for a new president. After reviewing the credentials of hundreds of candidates, the search came down to two finalists, with one as the definitely preferred person. His credentials appeared impeccable, his experience matched the position and his interview revealed an inspiring leader. The appointment seemed inevitable and imminent, but one member of the search committee asked that the decision be delayed for a day or two until all reference checks were in. On his résumé, the preferred candidate had listed a bachelor's degree in finance as his highest degree. But when the transcript was requested, the university of record reported that he had never graduated. When confronted with the question, he confessed that he had falsified his credentials. Needless to say, he lost the job and a promising future in banking.

Ironically, the second finalist who won the presidency and later advanced to the Chairman of the Board did not hold or claim a college degree. A small point? Perhaps, but the chief executive who is responsible for billions of dollars in assets must be trustworthy in the smallest things.

1. Assuming all other things equal, is integrity the bottom line of leadership, secular or Christian?

2. How can you test the integrity of a candidate as a part of the search and selection process?

3. If the personal or professional history of a candidate for leadership reveals an integrity lapse, can he or she be restored? On what conditions would you take the risk?

4. Is there a difference in the integrity of the Christian and secular leader? If so, how is it defined and tested?

5. What are some examples of integrity questions in the "gray areas" of secular fields? Should a Christian leader in a secular field err on the side of caution in these areas or is there a margin in which the "rules of the game" can be followed without spiritual detriment?

OUR INCARNATE MODEL
"EMPOWERING HIS PEOPLE"

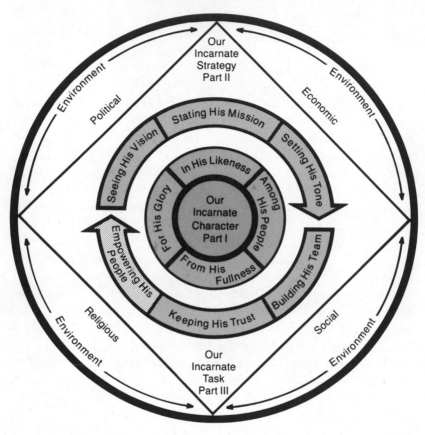

> But I tell you the truth: *It is for your*
> *good that I am going away.*
> John 16:7 NIV

12

Empowering His People

By the very nature of their role, Incarnate leaders must plan to make an exit. Because self-sacrifice is at the heart of the Incarnation, any number of reasons can bring its leadership to an end. For Jesus, His radical message and popular acceptance so threatened the entrenched religious establishment that their desperation drove them to shameful conspiracies, intolerable coalitions and, finally, the betrayal of a countryman into the hands of Gentiles, and Romans at that.

Other reasons for Incarnate leaders to exit from center stage include the completion of their task, such as in the case of John the Baptist, or expansion into new fields, such as the change of leadership from Peter to Paul in order to evangelize the Roman world. Whatever the case may be—age, completed task, expanded goals, changing times or martyrdom, the Incarnate leader must be ready and willing to make the personal sacrifice of stepping aside.

Jesus, of course, is our model for the Incarnational transfer. He died early to atone for the sins of humankind and entrusted world evangelization to His disciples.

John the Baptist is also our example. After preparing the way for Jesus, he saw his spectacular ministry fade into second place, his crowds defect to Jesus and his baptism by water superseded by the baptism of the Spirit.

If self-love, self-esteem or self-glory had ruled his heart, he would have cried "foul" and complained against the injustice of God. Instead, when he heard the word of Jesus' success, he exclaimed, "Now is my joy complete." No one better exemplifies the meaning of Incarnational transfer.

If every Incarnational leader must make an exit, preparation for the transfer of leadership to a successor or successors must also be made. Again, we look to Jesus to find working principles for succession.

Jesus' Incarnational Transfer

Preparation for the transfer of leadership is not a "crash program" that takes place just at the moment of change. From His first act of calling the fishermen, Peter, James and John, to discipleship, Jesus had succession in mind. Likewise, in the ongoing process of communicating His redemptive vision, modeling His servant mission and sounding His note of joy, His priority was the preparation of future leaders. Even more specifically, when He went about the task of organizing and developing His disciples, Jesus was counting upon them to carry out His mission. Without this long-term and advance preparation, the implementation of succession principles just before His departure would have been far less effective, if not impossible.

Still, there comes a time when the transfer of leadership has highest priority in a leader's career. As a cloud of doom settled over Jesus' destiny, it became obvious to all that His time had come. In his Gospel, John records the attention that Jesus gave to His disciples in preparation for His death and departure. Emotional preparation came first. After predicting His death and Peter's denial, Jesus must have sensed a despair that bordered on futility. So, with another display of a timely response, Jesus prepared the disciples for His absence by giving them the promise of being together again:

> Do not let your hearts be troubled. Trust in God; trust also in me. In my Father's house are many rooms; if it were not so, I would have told you. I am going there to prepare a place for you. And if I go and prepare a place for you, I will come back and take you to be with me that you also may be where I am. You know the way to the place where I am going.
>
> John 14:1–4 NIV

When Thomas demurs by saying "We don't know where you are going, so how can we know the way?" (John 14:5), Jesus answers with the call for trust: "I am the way, the truth and the life. No one comes to the Father except through me" (John 14:6).

As the conversation continues and Jesus reveals His intimate relationship with His Father, another reality surfaces. The disciples must be prepared for the hatred of the world. "Remember," Jesus says in paraphrase, "If the world hates you, keep in mind that it hated Me first" (John 15:18). Hatred, of course, will lead to persecution. In preparation for expulsion from the synagogue and betrayal at the hands of those who think that they are doing service to God, Jesus offers the reason and a warning:

> They will do such things because they have not known the Father or me. I have told you this, so that when the time comes you will remember that I warned you. I did not tell you this at first because I was with you.
>
> John 16:3–4 NIV

Interspersed between these three harsh realities—the absence of Jesus, the hatred of the world and the betrayal of religious leaders—are three separate promises for the coming of the Holy Spirit. Progressively, each promise becomes more specific and addresses the problems created by Jesus' departure:

FOR HIS ABSENCE—And I will ask the Father, and he will give you another Counselor to be with you forever—the Spirit of Truth. John 14:16–17 NIV

FOR THE HATRED OF THE WORLD—When the Counselor comes, whom I will send to you from the Father, the Spirit of Truth who goes out from the Father, he will testify about me. And you also must testify, for you have been with me from the beginning. John 15:26–27 NIV

FOR THE BETRAYAL OF RELIGIOUS LEADERS—When he (the Counselor) comes, he will convict the world of guilt in regard to sin and righteousness and judgment: in regard to righteousness, because I am going to the Father, where you can see me no longer; and in regard to judgment, because the prince of this world now stands condemned. John 16:8–11 NIV

Never dodging the truth, Jesus tells the disciples that they will go through a period of weeping and mourning while the world rejoices at His death. But through the presence and promise of the Holy Spirit, He assures them, ". . . your grief will turn to joy" (John 16:20). With the fulfillment of that promise, the Incarnational cycle will be complete. Meanwhile, the promise serves as part of the emotional preparation of the disciples. Though they despair of His departure, they can anticipate His joy.

Spiritual preparation for succession came next. Jesus prayed that His disciples would bear His name and speak His Word just as He had been faithful to the name and Word of God the Father. By bearing His name, Jesus prayed for the same unity among them that He had known with His Father; by speaking His Word, Jesus prayed for the same joy that He found in doing His Father's will. But prayer was not enough. Jesus knew the hazards of sending His disciples into the world just as His Father had sent Him into the world. To back up His prayer that they might be set apart by truth and protected from the temptations of Satan, Jesus renewed His Incarnational commitment, "For them I sanctify myself, that they too may be truly sanctified" (John 17:19 NIV).

After this prayer for the spiritual preparation of His successors, Jesus went into the Garden of Gethsemane where His passion began in one last soul-struggle with the temptation of self-preservation or the "will to live." Out of that experience came the decisive words that finalized forever His Incarnate purpose, "Not my will, but yours be done." Betrayal, arrest, trial, crucifixion and resurrection followed, not independent of the succession process. Through these experiences and the miracles that followed, John reports:

> . . . these are written that you may believe that Jesus is the Christ, the Son of God, and that by believing you may have life in His name.
>
> John 20:31 NIV

Naming His Backup

After the Resurrection, Jesus returns to the task of transferring leadership to His disciples. His first priority is the reinstatement of Peter through the test of unconditional love. Walking him back through the steps of his denial, Jesus asks Peter three times, "Do you love me?" In response, Peter acts as if Jesus is asking a rhetorical question, "Lord, You know I love You." Each time results in a leadership commission, "Feed my lambs," "Take care of my sheep" and "Feed my sheep." Jesus then tells Peter how He will die to glorify God and concludes with the repetition of His first call to Peter, "Follow me."

Although Jesus leaves no doubt about Peter's restored role as first-in-command, one last moment of "storming" arises between him and John. In a personalized parenthesis to his Gospel, John notes that a rumor had spread that he alone

164 ~ OUR INCARNATE TASK

among the disciples would not die. If true, it meant that John must have had special status with Jesus. So, Peter asks, "Lord, what about him?" With eternal patience, Jesus answers, "If I want him to remain alive until I return, what is that to you? You must follow me."

The essence of Incarnational leadership is here revealed. To lead others is to follow Jesus to the death without regard for competitive status or comparative roles. Peter is appointed to lead, but not yet anointed to lead. He needs the baptism of the Holy Spirit to become an Incarnational leader in the likeness of Christ, among His people, through His fullness and for His glory.

Extending His Strategy

Jesus' vision "to seek and save the lost" has now become fully operative through His death and Resurrection. It will guide the strategy for succession. Meeting the eleven disciples on the top of the mountain in Galilee, Jesus gives the Great Commission as the strategy for implementing the extension of His redemptive vision to include the whole world for all generations to come. Here again, we discover a mission statement with all the components that a leader needs to motivate followers, mobilize resources and monitor performance.

Authority:	The Name of Jesus
Timing:	Urgency
Task:	Make disciples
Geography:	All nations
Symbol:	Baptism
Skill:	Teaching
Subject:	The Word of Christ
Outcome:	Obedience to commands of Christ
Promise:	Christ's presence
Term:	To the very end of the age

Matthew 28:16–20

Notable in the strategy is the leadership task of making disciples. Evangelization often dead-ends on the goal of winning souls. What is intended to be an ever-expanding and yet integrated network gets stopped by enclaves and empires that are self-contained if not self-serving. The task of discipling, however, is modeled after Jesus' recruitment, organization and extension of those whom He called to follow Him. The twelve were divided into teams of two in order to lead teams of twelve with a long-term view toward an exponential network for world evangelization. In other words, every component of strategy in the Great Commission is a direct extension of Jesus' Incarnational leadership. It is the game-plan for fulfilling the Incarnational strategy, transferring the Incarnational task and implementing the succession of Incarnational leadership. Pure and simple, it means that every Christian is a leader and a follower at the same time.

Empowering His Successors

One element of the Incarnational transfer is missing. The disciples have the promise of the continuing Presence of Christ, the appointment of Peter as the leader among leaders and the strategy of the Great Commission for fulfilling the redemptive vision. They lack the power of the Holy Spirit. As we have repeated so many times, at each critical juncture in leadership development, the work of the Holy Spirit is essential. Because Incarnation is a paradox between divine and human factors which can never be reconciled by human effort, only the Holy Spirit can bring about the creative synthesis that will unify the disciples as an inspired and innovative missionary team. When Jesus told them that He was going away for their good, He meant that His Presence could be in each of them as a gift of the Holy Spirit.

Furthermore, according to the Incarnational principle, the empowerment of others comes from the example of the leader's self-sacrifice. With the Great Commission, the disciples received their appointment to a holy task; with the baptism of the Spirit, they were anointed with the power to perform that task. After Pentecost, the apostles could say the same thing that Jesus said in His inaugural sermon when He announced His strategy for mission, "The Spirit of the Lord is upon me, he has anointed me . . . ." In this context, we understand the meaning of the common question which the apostles asked their converts, "Have you received the Holy Ghost since you believed?" The baptism of the Holy Spirit brought the presence and power of Jesus Christ into the life of the believer. Once again, it could be said, "The Word became flesh . . . ."

So, as the final instruction in the transfer of Incarnate leadership from Jesus Christ to the apostles, He commanded them:

> Do not leave Jerusalem, but wait for the gift my Father promised, which you have heard me speak about. For John baptized with water, but in a few days you will be baptized with the Holy Spirit:
>
> Acts 1:4–5 NIV

Still trapped in a narrow human and political perspective, the apostles assumed that Jesus meant that He would restore the kingdom of Israel. Without denying that the restoration is part of His long-range purpose, Jesus tells them the real purpose of the baptism of the Holy Spirit:

> . . . you will receive power when the Holy Spirit comes on you; and you will be my witnesses in Jerusalem, and in all Judea and Samaria, and to the ends of the earth.
>
> Acts 1:8 NIV

For the first time, the promise of power is added to the promise of His presence. But we must not forget that the power is given for one specific purpose—to witness of the Presence of Christ in a strategy that begins at Jerusalem and extends in concentric circles through Judea, Samaria and to the outer edges of the earth. With amazing congruence, the geographic strategy complements organizational strategy. As the disciples were organized to lead multiplying teams of twelve into a world-embracing network, the web of their witness began in Jerusalem and reached out in expanding steps until the gospel was heard at the ends of the earth.

When the apostles were baptized by the Holy Spirit, the Incarnational transfer was complete. Christ now entrusted His redemptive vision, strategic mission and organizational plan to the team of disciples whom He had prepared for leadership. Not by kind, but by degree, He saw in them the potential for doing greater things than He had done. With the empowerment of His disciples at Pentecost, Jesus must have said, "Now is My joy complete."

Taking Our Leave

Sooner or later, a leader has to leave. Timing is crucial. Some leaders overstay their time; others move too quickly. For Incarnate leaders, the Holy Spirit serves as timekeeper. Sometimes He only needs to give us a nudge; at other times it takes a shove. Through experience and observation, I have become a student of timing for leadership change.

My interest in timing began when I heard a professor say that great leaders know when to make their exit. Soon after this, my father-in-law reached the age of sixty-five and had to make the decision to retire from the pastoral ministry or move to another parish. For more than forty years, he had served with great honor and love as a pastor and leader for the denomination. But behind the pending move was an edge of criticism that could magnify in the years ahead. When he asked me, his brash young son-in-law, what he should do, I answered, "Retire, Dad. You and Mom deserve some years together in the first home you have ever owned." Whether or not my advice made the difference is incidental. Dad and Mom retired to their little cottage and lived into their nineties with an ever-growing aura of love and honor for their ministry.

A few years later, a prominent editor had the option of being elected for another four-year term that would have taken him into his seventies. He qualified for another term by the accident of a birthday that came just a few days before the date when he would have been ineligible. Hoping for support to run again, he talked with many people, including me. When I heard his story, I realized that he wanted to run again for the wrong reasons. He had tied his ego to the job so tightly that he would suffocate it in the next four years. So I told him the story of my father-in-law and then recommended, "Retire. Young people like me need you as our elder statesman." He retired and at the age of eighty-seven has just completed another book for which I wrote the foreword.

Incarnational principles have a bearing upon the timing for taking our leave from leadership. Foremost, of course, is obedience to the will of God. By nature, I am an ambitious and impatient person, more entrepreneurial than managerial. Like everyone else, I love to be courted for a new position. Sometimes I drop hints about being open to change if the right position came along. On one or two occasions, I have even tried to turn handles and force open doors of opportunity that appeared to be closed. But when the bottom line is drawn, I ask the question, "Is this the will of God for me?" Because my prior commitment is to obey God, I have never made a move that did not have a sense of closure and clearance in His good will.

Closely related to our obedience is our task. In His final report to His Father, Jesus said, "I have finished the work that you gave me to do" (John 17:4 NIV). It is an error to assume that every leadership position is scheduled for a lifetime. Each situation is different. Some tasks are short-term, others are long-term. After I completed my doctorate in my middle twenties, I forecast my career in five-year blocks of time. Every five years I would point toward a promotion or a move. It worked, give or take a year or two, during the first three promotions or moves in my career. Then, after five years at Seattle Pacific University, I faced the question of whether or not to make a move. In counsel with Kenneth Hansen, Chairman of Servicemaster at the time, I had my perspective changed. Mr. Hansen said that leaders need about four or five years to develop programs in institutions, but it takes seven years or more to develop people. His words were wise. Looking back upon my career, I saw the tracks of innovative programs, capital projects, fiscal stability and academic recognition. Looking deeper, I realized that the people whom I had influenced during my career represented the value I prized as permanent. Consequently, I stayed at Seattle Pacific University for a double term of fourteen years.

No set formula can guide the time that leaders take their leave. Some are called short-term to develop programs; others are called long-term to develop people. Still others are called into transitional positions between long-term leaders. As a rule of thumb is that long-term leaders, especially those who have become legends, will be followed by a series of short-termers who fail or are frustrated because of comparisons with their predecessor. John Wooden, The Wizard of Westwood, who won eleven unprecedented national basketball championships at UCLA, is the best example. Five or six basketball coaches have come and gone since Wooden's retirement. The question is not competency, but comparison. Unrealistic expectations have greeted each new coach as alumni and fans failed to realize that the circumstances which contributed to Wooden's success have changed. UCLA no longer has the corner on recruiting top-quality athletes in Southern California. Without taking anything away from the genius of John Wooden, he came and left at the right time.

In contrast, I think of a pastor who served a church for twenty-three years with legendary stature. He moved at the right time as the expectations of the congregation began to change. When it happened, I predicted that his successor would be short-term because of comparison, particularly in preaching. A bishop's wise decision made my prediction both true and false. He appointed a pastor who was strong where the former pastor was criticized. More importantly, he appointed him with the mutual understanding that he would be short-term and retire after four years. His transitional ministry proved to be most effective. When he retired in four years, the climate of comparison no longer existed. His successor, whose style would have been criticized four years earlier, came in with freedom from comparative expectations.

At the national level, I have always felt that Gerald Ford would have been remembered as a great president if he had accepted the transitional role as a "healer" after Watergate. Instead, when he decided to run for election in 1976, he lost because he overextended his gifts and overstayed his time.

Incarnational leadership puts a premium upon the timing for taking our leave. Our gifts must match the needs of the people whom we serve. Organizations have personalities as well as leaders. They also go through cycles of change which call for differing kinds of leadership gifts. Visionary leaders are needed at one time, strategic planners at another and operational managers at still another time. For us, the key is knowing how and when we fit. Peter Drucker suggests that leaders should periodically ask themselves three questions regarding their organization and its needs:

- What needs to be done?
- Can I do it?
- Do I want to do it?

Most of us are not leaders for all seasons. Even Jesus, with His uncanny sense of timing, knew when to make His exit. Putting aside self-love, self-esteem and self-glory, He prepared His successors and sacrificed Himself for the larger good and the greater glory of God.

Advancing Our Strategy

As difficult as it may seem, taking our leave may advance our strategy for servanthood. If we assume that we are servants of God, owning nothing, but stewards of all He has put into our trust, we must see our leadership continuing after we leave. Jesus gives us our Incarnational example. He left for the good of His disciples and the advancement of his mission. Brutally put, the Great Commission could not have been activated or accomplished if Jesus had not returned to His Father.

After taking our leave, we must get out of the way. Tragedy stalks individuals and institutions where former leaders stand in the light of their successors. In one case, I was called by the Secretary of the Board of Trustees asking if I were interested in the presidency of a nationally recognized university. Flattered, but confused, I asked what happened to the former president whom I knew as a strong leader in educational circles. The answer came back that he would become Chancellor with responsibility for relationships with the church and the community.

"To whom does he report?" I asked. Hesitating, the caller answered, "This hasn't been decided yet. I assume that he will report to the Board of Trustees."

All my experience with two-headed monsters in other organizations collapsed upon me. Thanking her for the call, I concluded the conversation and closed the door on the opportunity by saying, "Let me know when you have made that decision. It will determine whether or not I am interested."

She never called back and I predicted a short-term disaster for the person who took the position. Sure enough, an outstanding educator lasted less than two years. Crucifixion is the best description for his demise and many years later the institution still has not recovered.

Getting Out of the Way

On the other hand, I have a model of an Incarnational leader who taught me how to leave and get out of the way. At Seattle Pacific University, I succeeded Dr. Dorr Demaray in the presidency. Our styles are just the opposite. He is one of the most gentle and spiritual persons I have ever known. In contrast, I have the reputation for a tough mind, and occasionally a tender heart. With dignity and honor

Dr. Demaray presided over the growth years of the school during the 1960s. At the end of the decade, the tide turned. For the private sector of higher education, funds dried up, enrollments fell and expansion stopped. Dire predictions were made about the future. Coming to retirement age, President Demaray voluntarily took his leave, knowing that a new era demanded new leadership.

When I took the position, he debriefed me without a bad word for anyone and then said, "If I can help, let me know. Otherwise, I'm going to get out of your way. I have other things to do." He meant it. For the next twenty years, he led annual trips to the Holy Land, founded mission schools in Hong Kong, responded to world-wide speaking invitations and served the church and community on multiple boards and committees. Whenever we met, he commended me on my leadership and spoke with pride about the changes in the University. Dorr Demaray is a model of the Incarnate leader who takes his leave, gets out of the way and finds joy in the advancement of the mission after he is gone.

I found myself being just the opposite one day when I revisited Spring Arbor College where I served as president. Walking across the campus, I met the superintendent of buildings and grounds whom I had hired. Warmly, we shook hands and I asked the standard question, "How are things going?" His eyes lit up and he exclaimed, "Great! Things are *better than ever* now." To him, I answered, "Good," but inside, I pouted, "How can things be better than ever now? I'm not here."

The Spirit of God checked my resentment and made me realize that the world does not revolve around my feverish little ego. Since then, I have tried to encourage my successors and commend the advancements of the schools where I have served. In place of resentment, there is joy.

Leaving Our Legacy

Another Incarnational principle arises out of these experiences. The full effectiveness of leadership cannot be determined until after the leader leaves. History itself will judge the clarity of the vision, the effectiveness of the mission and the quality of the tone that the leader leaves behind. More and more, I am convinced that organizations have personalities which persist over a long period of time. Leaders can only change the nuances of that personality. Yet those changes will also persist over time, slowly reshaping the personality of the institution. This is why the Incarnational leader must also be satisfied with "small wins" that contribute to the big picture which only history can reveal.

At Asbury Theological Seminary, for instance, I have seen the history of the institution written through the personalities of its presidents. Henry Clay Morrison, a pathfinding pioneer with a vision of "spreading scriptural holiness across the land," founded the Seminary. J. C. McPheeters followed him with a strategy of prayer and preaching that resulted in revival. Frank Bateman Stanger succeeded McPheeters with a strong sense of churchmanship and the gift for setting a pastoral tone. Asbury today is an Incarnational blend of these leaders—a vision of scriptural holiness, a strategy for world evangelism and a tone of pastoral care. Their legacy gives our generation the base upon which to build for the future.

Incarnational leaders are more concerned about the base they leave upon which others build than they are about the achievements they can claim. One of the differences between Christian and secular leaders is the emphasis upon achievement and success. As evident in the Great Commission, the task of Christian leadership is to develop disciples who will be the means for evangelizing the world. The results belong to the Holy Spirit and the glory belongs to God. So, the legacy of the Incarnate leader is to build a base upon the foundations of the past with an eye to the future. Jesus built this base in His career so that the strategy of the Great Commission unleashed the potential of His disciples to do greater things than He had done. Here we may have discovered the final and most critical test for Incarnational leadership. *Do we leave a foundation from which those who follow us can do greater things than we have done?*

Usually it is awkward for a departing leader to propose the strategy for the future of the organization. Once a resignation or retirement is announced, all parties tend to become emotionally detached in a "lame duck" setting. But who better can draw from the perspective of the past and project into the future? It is not a matter of imposing the personality of the past leader upon the future one, but rather an unusual opportunity to tap the wisdom of experience once it has been objectified by impending departure. If I were a trustee of an institution or the director of an organization, I would consider a strategic debriefing with the departing leader as essential to my responsibility for choosing the next leaders whose gifts match the goals for the future. Incarnational leaders build upon the past and build for the future.

Preparing Our Team

People are more important than program in the legacy of the Incarnational leader. Jesus left a team of disciples in whom His redemptive vision, servant mission and joyful tone were internalized as working values. He went one step farther. In preparation for His departure, He restored His relationship with Peter and reappointed Him to be executive in His absence. Another task in the transfer of leadership is revealed. Incarnational leaders prepare backup leadership just as Jesus prepared Peter.

As fundamental as it may seem, few leaders prepare backup persons for their role. Consequently, when either death, illness, resignation or retirement requires a change of leadership, the organization slumps into a vacuum and boards start the frantic search for names. This is a sensitive area because any hint of preselection of a successor by departing leadership is met with strong, if not bitter, resistance. Yet, if we follow the principle of Incarnational transfer demonstrated by Jesus, we cannot forfeit our responsibility to prepare backup leadership whether or not the person is elected to succeed us.

A sabbatical period is one way to test your team. During my career, I have had three sabbaticals ranging from six weeks to three months. After thoroughly briefing my leadership team on procedures for handling on-going operations as well as crises, my instruction is, "Don't call me and I won't call you." Of course, I am available for counsel in crisis, but even then, I leave the decision with the chief executive in my absence and the executive team. More than the team is tested. It can be a threat to realize that the organization can run without you. It is even more of a threat to think that no one cares. At present, I am on sabbatical and I find the most precious words in cards or calls to be, "We miss you." The human side of Incarnational leadership cannot be denied.

In addition to preparing a person to back up our leadership for transition, team preparation is necessary. Jesus prepared His disciples emotionally and spiritually for His departure by assuring them of the larger purpose that would be accomplished. Of course, He could comfort them by the promise of heaven and His eternal presence. But the greater promise was the quality of the relationship they would have with Him and together in the present world. Not unlike the relationship He knew with His Father, they would know the same love, joy and peace which characterized the inner strength and vibrancy of Jesus. Leaving is always hard and usually bittersweet. Words of comfort are helpful, but not as meaningful as the relationships that continue on a new and different level. Years after leaving a place, I meet administrators, faculty and students with whom I was associated and find a special camaraderie that draws us together. Most surprising and rewarding are the foes who have become fast friends.

Empowering Our Successors

All the preparation for the transfer of leadership has one goal: *to empower our successors*. Although the Holy Spirit is the agent of Incarnational empowerment, the Christian leader still serves as a model in the process. When Jesus ascended into heaven His disciples were not yet ready to assume leadership for the Great Commission. Some believed and others doubted. They lacked courage. The fear of the Jews still kept them cowering behind closed doors. They lacked creativity. Although they had the satisfaction of "small wins" in their internship, they had never tested their skills in a setting independent of Jesus. So, for them to lead, He had to leave.

Anticipation is another outcome of Incarnational leadership. Jesus knew that after He left, the disciples would naturally look backward to the memories of their glory days with the Savior. So, when He left, He instructed them to wait together in the Upper Room until they were empowered from on high. Once He got them looking forward, He knew that the coming of the Holy Spirit would unify them to follow Him, inspire them to lead His church and energize them to win the world. By sacrificing Himself and leaving them, Jesus prepared the way for their empowerment.

Incarnational transfer of leadership has the empowerment of others as its goal. When a leader leaves, people should come together rather than breaking apart, rise to the challenge of leadership themselves and find creative ways to get on with the job. This will not happen by accident. Preparation for empowerment will come from the sense of anticipation which the departing leader leaves behind. Then, following the leader's example of self-sacrifice for their sake, the successors will be empowered by the Holy Spirit with His unifying, encouraging and creative Presence.

Some leaders may embarrass rather than empower their successors. Several times during my career, I have been asked to assume presidencies or positions which might be considered competitive or downgrading for the institution I would leave. In one case, I was invited to consider the presidency of a Christian liberal arts college in the same region of the country where I had served as president of a competitive school. Categorically, I turned down the invitation with the explanation that I would do nothing to compete with whatever contribution I had made to the other institution in the past.

On another occasion, the call came to consider an institution of the same type in another part of the country from the one I served. The offer had some intrigue because of its innovative nature, but such a move would have been interpreted as a put-down for the institution where I currently served. I said, "No."

When Incarnational leadership comes to its final test, the question is whether or not our leaving leads to the empowerment of our successors. If we have communicated our vision clearly, they will come together in unity around that dream. If we have modeled our strategy for servanthood effectively, they will be inspired to rise to new levels of leadership. If we have set the tone of joy in our leadership, they will sing as they lead. If and when this happens through the empowerment of the Holy Spirit, our Incarnational transfer will be complete, the Incarnational process will have come full circle, and the "mind of Christ" will be in us as well as in those who have followed us.

Case in Point

Two distinguished professors had lifetime careers in Christian higher education. Wherever alumni of their institutions gathered, they asked first about these professors and recalled their intellectual and spiritual influence upon student lives.

At the time of their retirement, a difference in their influence came to light. In advance of their retirement, a search began for their replacements. For one professor, no former students could be identified who had taken advanced graduate study in the field to replace the teacher. But for the other professor, the search produced six candidates who either had completed doctorates or were in the final stages of the degree. In addition, an equal number of former students were already in the teaching field and qualified for the position. The difference is puzzling.

1. If empowering others to lead is the goal of Incarnational Christian leadership, did the one professor fail at this point? Or is empowerment expressed in many dimensions?

2. Is discipling natural to leadership or must it be more intentional?

3. Think again about the most effective leaders you have known. Are disciples who can replace them and excel beyond them one of the proofs of their greatness?

4. Recall your own leadership role—whether long or short term. Have you taught disciples who could succeed you? Among your accomplishments, is the empowerment of others one of your most meaningful and lasting rewards?

13

Epilogue:
Who Will Follow Him?

We began with the question, "Who will lead us into the twenty-first century?" An answer is already being formulated in the corporate world. *U. S. News and World Report* (March 7, 1988) has featured as its cover story "The Twenty-First Century Executive."[1] According to the article, the leader of the future must be: (1) a *global strategist*—with the understanding and skills to negotiate across world cultures; (2) a *master of technology*—with a working knowledge of the potential of scientific research and development; (3) a *politician par excellence*—with the skills to steer through the morass of governmental regulations and public pressures; and (4) a *leader-facilitator*—with the moxie and charisma to persuade others to make a commitment to shared values.

Most notable in this profile of the twenty-first century executive is the absence of a mission beyond the profit motive; a morality beyond the negotiating context; and a model beyond professional skills. Still, the profile has meaning for Christian leadership in the twenty-first century. For one thing, it serves

179

fair warning that we cannot prepare Christians to lead in a world that no longer exists. To drive into the future with our eyes on the rear view mirror is to miss the redemptive vision which can only be seen by looking ahead. More than that, the profile has meaning because the four qualifications for the twenty-first century executive arise out of paradoxes which can become opportunities for Incarnational leadership.

The Paradox of Perspective

The expectation that the twenty-first century executive will be a *global strategist* poses the paradox of perspective. At the same time that the leader of the future must see the global potential, whether for marketing or missions, local responsibility cannot be forgotten. When one begins to think in global terms his mind fills up with exotic promises and faraway places. After all, the Great Commission is a global strategy and vital Christianity always has a world compassion. Yet, few of us know the full implications of the Great Commission as a global strategy. Our world perspective, at best, tends to be selective and impersonal—selective in the sense that we limit the field of our compassion by maintaining our cultural superiority and impersonal in the sense that we write checks rather than giving ourselves. To disturb the comfort of our ingrained ethnocentricity is a traumatic exercise.

The corporate world is already ahead of us. Driven by the profit motive and foreseeing a world economy, there is no alternative to a "global strategy" to survive in the twenty-first century. Some time ago I discovered the book entitled *The World Class Executive.*[2] It is a working manual for cross-cultural organization, management and marketing. As I read the book, I found myself substituting the words "witness" for "sales" and "evangelism" for "marketing." Not that a secular field motivated by profit should dictate our understanding of Christian missions. The Incarnational motive is missing. But for cross-cultural sensitivity, *The World Class Executive* reads like an orientation manual for missionary candidates.

The threat as well as the opportunity of a global perspective is evident in our response to television pictures of world suffering. Scenes of hollow-eyed babies with bloated stomachs have an immediate emotional impact upon us and may prompt a gift to a relief organization. But without personal engagement in the suffering, we quickly retreat into the cocoon of our comfort rather than developing a long-term, in-depth commitment to global needs. In fact, our perspective narrows rather than widens as we turn inwardly to protect ourselves from the sight of suffering.

This strange reversal has been documented in a study on the attitudes of college students sponsored by the Carnegie Commission for the Advancement of Teaching.[3] Contrary to expectations, students today are not developing a global perspective. They see world-suffering and witness world events instantaneously in living color. Yet they do not respond. Self-interest squeezes them into the tight circle of their own aspirations. Consequently, they lack a concern for their local community as much as for their world community. Self-interest cuts both ways. Civic responsibility at home cannot be separated from civic responsibility abroad.

Christians are not without fault at this point. By and large, we tend to be more concerned about global needs than we are about local problems. The plea of Rachel in Koskol's book, *Rachel and Her Children*, still rings in my ears. When speaking about our compassion for the hungry and homeless overseas, Rachel cries, "How come you care so much for people you can't see? Ain't we the world? Ain't we a piece of it?"[4]

Out of this grim reality arises an Incarnational opportunity for Christian leaders. Through the eyes of the spirit and the insights of the mind of Christ, we can develop a global perspective consistent with the strategy of the Great Commission. Beginning at home in our own "Jerusalem" where we learn the meaning of compassion and responsibility, we can then move cross-culturally into Judea, Samaria and "away to the ends of the earth."

In other words, the Christian leader of the future who is a *"global strategist"* will teach and model civic responsibility at home as preparation for Christian citizenship in the world at large. First and foremost, our strategy must be proactive, enterprising and innovative—seeking the lost in places where the gospel has not been preached or among people for whom the gospel has not been applied. At the same time, our strategy must be guided by the Holy Spirit. Self-interest must go and self-giving must come. An Incarnational leader will be a global strategist for the redemptive vision at home and abroad.

The Paradox of Resources

Tension between human and technical resources has been present from the time of the invention of the earliest machine. In the future, however, that tension will be aggravated by the speed and impact of high technology. For this reason, the twenty-first century executive is expected to be a *master of technology*. But what about human resources? Tension pulls us into the paradox of resources. Which will have priority? Which has greater potential? Which will be our master and which will be our slave? High technology or common humanity?

The speed and impact of advancing technology is a grim reality for the future. When we talk about "high technology" we are referring to the mind-boggling level of sophistication and exponential speed of new inventions. Imagine what is called a "J" curve. Technology begins on the baseline of the "J" until inventions come together in a synergistic effect and multiply exponentially on a rising and speeding line of discovery up the stem of the "J." The shape of the "J" shows us how technology can spiral out of control, especially if technicians in research and development assume the attitude, "whatever can be done must be done." Human beings, then, can become slaves rather than masters of technology.

Critics, such as Jacques Ellul, foresee the "demonic" in uncontrolled technological advance, anticipating not so much that it is possessed by Satan, but rather that it will become a dominant force in human behavior. Already, in the field of ethics, we are playing a catch-up game with scientific advancement. Fertility drugs, for example, are encouraged by pro-lifers as a counterforce to abortion. Yet, when the drug works too well, multiple children in a single pregnancy result and an ethical dilemma develops. How many fetuses need to be aborted in order to save others and protect the life of the mother?

More complicated yet is the question, "Which fetuses do we abort?" As medical science advances, early diagnosis will predict the characteristics of the fetuses so that decisions will have to be made either by random choice or by sex, strength and potential for the quality of life. The grim reality is that advancing technology will create human complexities and moral ambiguities far beyond our wildest imagination in the years ahead. Even more than a master of technology, the Incarnate Christian leader will have to be a master of human resources and moral issues.

The Paradox of Politics

The importance attached to the twenty-first century executive as a *politician par excellence* introduces a third grim and good reality about the future which we cannot ignore. Partially as a result of advancing technology and partially as a product of the changing social structure, interaction between institutions and individuals is becoming increasingly political. Most evident are government regulations regarding health, safety and human welfare which will fall like a net over every sphere of our relationships—local, regional, national and international. Not by coincidence, while writing these words, I heard the mailman arrive with the daily mail. When I went downstairs to check the letters, on top of the pile was the blue-and-white government booklet that has been mailed to every household in the nation under the title "Understanding AIDS." The crisis created by this dread disease, which knows no boundaries of place, class, color, sex, origin or creed, signals the future of governmental involvement in regulatory action, educational prevention and medical intervention in our lives. The threat is real; the options are limited.

Still another area which calls for leaders who are *politicians par excellence* is the litigious climate which involves the issues of individual rights. Whether we like it or not, a radical swing has moved us from institutional control to individual rights. Not by coincidence, the day after the "Understanding AIDS" booklet arrived, the report of the Presidential AIDS Commission came out with the centerpiece recommendation that the federal government take strong action to assure AIDS victims against discrimination in such areas as education, employment, housing and public services. However we may feel about such regulation is incidental to the fact that the federal government is called upon to protect individual rights in a controversial field where facts are still limited.

Christian leaders will confront their own particular form of legislation, regulation and litigation in the area of church-state relationships. The stage has already been set by cases in the late 1980s in a more conservative political climate. Issues range far and wide:

. . . Is it constitutional for a city to erect a Christmas creche on the courthouse lawn?
. . . Can a religious organization discriminate in hiring practices by requiring that employees be committed Christians?
. . . Does financial aid given to students in a Christian college require compliance with equal opportunity regulations throughout the institution?
. . . Is the tax-exempt status on the property of religious institutions a public expenditure which should be reviewed?
. . . Can the IRS determine what is a tax-deductible "ministry" for a Christian organization?

. . . Should regulations and audits of fund-raising activities in Christian organizations be required to avoid abuses?

. . . Can a local ordinance banning discrimination against homosexuals take precedence over the first amendment for Christian institutions?

The list could go on and on. Discerning scholars predict that church-state conflicts will dominate our legal agenda into the twenty-first century. Yet, the issues are not new. Gustad, in his book *Faith of Our Fathers*, reminds us that church-state issues stood at the center of controversy in the founding of our nation. While categorically rejecting the notion of a national church, our founding fathers recognized the need for the church and its people ". . . to ensure community and commonwealth and commitment."[5] Most surprising, even those founding fathers whom we do not immediately identify with the faith—such as Adams and Jefferson—readily agreed with the historian Alexis de Tocqueville that the Church had to be "regularly purified and renewed" in order to fulfill its spiritual task "to counter selfishness and pride" and its political task ". . . to repeatedly and emphatically distinguish between those loyalties due an all-sovereign God and those due an all-fallible nation."[6]

Once again, an Incarnational paradox confronts us. Christian leaders of the future, as their predecessors in the past, will have to ride the line of tension between the spiritual and political purpose of the Church and its people. Ralph Waldo Emerson, the transcendentalist, saw the role of Christian leaders most clearly in his day when he said that the "dangers and dragons" which beset our young nation could not be met by "dunces and idlers."[7] Gustad's last sentence in his book *Faith of Our Fathers* is to say that the challenge has not changed. "Neither dunces nor idlers could do much about dangers and dragons in those days, nor—one suspects—in our own."[8]

Most important of all, Christian leaders must be gatekeepers against the temptation to seek political solutions for spiritual problems. However good and noble our political efforts may be, they must never take precedence over spiritual regeneration. John Wesley set the standard for us in the eighteenth century. Although England was corrupt to its cultural core, Wesley resisted the pressure to be identified as a social reformer until the Methodist movement had credibility as a spiritual force for personal redemption throughout the nation. By holding his position for the redemptive strategy, Wesley saw both the results of regeneration and reform. An Incarnate Christian leader of the twenty-first century will face the same test.

The Paradox of Power

The leadership style of the twenty-first century executive as a *leader-facilitator* carries its own paradox—the paradox of power. Without question, the power once centralized in traditional hierarchies is being distributed to stakeholders throughout our organizations. The hyphenated term "leader-facilitator" accurately reflects the changing power scene and the ensuing Incarnational paradox. The "leader" side of the hyphen implies the authority of command based upon position while the "facilitator" side of the hyphen infers the authority of person and the power of persuasion. Taking metaphors from athletics or music, "coach" or "conductor" are good descriptions of the changing leadership role. In both cases, the authority of the leader and the power of the "last word" form the baseline for effective results. Yet, if the performance of either the athletic team or the symphony orchestra is to rise to the level of championship play or artistic excellence, it will be because the leader is able to motivate the performers by the "power" of personal and persuasive inspiration.

Throughout the book we have avoided the use of the word "power" because it carries so much negative freight in the minds of people, especially the young. We cannot avoid the term any longer. Like it or not, "power" to influence the behavior of followers is the essential ingredient in leadership. Of course, power can be abused and corrupted. But it can also be as spiritually effective and humanly enhancing as the power that Jesus promised His disciples at Pentecost. In fact, without the inspiration and authority of that power to lead, Christianity would have been stalled as a world movement and Jesus Christ would have been discredited as the Son of God. So, the question is not whether Incarnate Christian leaders exercise power but what kind of power is exercised? From what source? And to what end?

Management literature describes four kinds of power: *position* power, *expert* power, *coercive* power, and *referent* power. Depending upon the circumstances, a leader will exercise all four kinds of power from time to time. Perhaps the key to effective leadership is knowing when to use which kind of power with whom in a given situation. The style of leaders tends to be identified by the kind of power upon which they rely. Some rely on the power of their position; others on their expertise in a given field; others on the ability to coerce by rewards and punishments—and still others by the force of their personality or the quality of their character.

Jesus drew the contrast between the spiritual and secular use of power when He reminded His ambitious disciples of the rulers of Gentiles who "lord it over" their people (Matthew 20:24–28). Coercive power is implied. To back up coercive power, a system of rewards and punishments is needed. Yet, rewards and punishments represent the least effective form of power for changing behavior and growing people. The reason is that rewards and punishments must be constantly reinforced and escalated. Behavior may be controlled by these means of coercive power, but people will not be positively and permanently changed.

In the same breath that He rejects coercive power, Jesus gives His disciples the model of servant-power with Himself as the example. In one sense, servant-power is a category of influence outside the four traditional kinds of power. Servanthood is a leadership style which relies upon the power of self-giving without self-glory. Such power is possible only through the work of the Holy Spirit. Otherwise, servanthood rapidly degenerates into a form of manipulation which can be more subtly coercive than coercive power itself. Servanthood, as a leadership style, depends upon referent power in a spiritual context.

We find ourselves back where we started—at the character of the leader. Although the *U. S. News and World Report* article neglects this factor, for Incarnational Christian leadership it is both the starting point and the stopping place for our study. We cannot pose the question, "Who will lead us?" without asking in the same breath, "Who will follow Him?" Instantly, His Incarnate character, strategy and task come before us once again and we find ourselves face-to-face with the larger questions:

Who will *embody* His Spirit?
Who will *embrace* His vision?
Who will *empower* His people?

A Spiritual View

Quite in contrast with the qualifications for future leadership outlined in the *U. S. News and World Report* is the spiritual profile filled out by Henri Nouwen in his book *In the Name of Jesus: Reflections on the Future of Christian Leadership.* Whereas the profile in *U. S. News and World Report* is developed from an external "environmental scan" and focuses upon the functional role of future leadership, Nouwen creates his profile out of an internal "personal scan" with a focus upon spiritual relationships. Nouwen's profile for the Christian leader of the future has three characteristics: (a) a praying leader; (b) a vulnerable leader; and (c) a trusting leader.[9] Although these spiritual credentials may not be as specific as the functional qualities of the twenty-first century executive, they become specific under the skillful pen of Nouwen—so specific, in fact, that he leaves you well aware of your spiritual shortcomings and with full knowledge of what you must do to qualify as a Christian leader. After reading Nouwen, we realize that he has penetrated through to the place where Incarnational leadership begins—embodying the praying, vulnerable and trusting Spirit of Jesus Christ. In these qualities we find the resolution for the paradox between our functional responsibilities and our spiritual qualities as Christian leaders.

The Resolution of Incarnate Love

A *praying leader,* according to Nouwen, is needed for the future in order to resist the ever-increasing temptation *"to be relevant."* Every leader knows the pressure to be competent in providing answers to questions, clarity to issues, solutions to problems and resolutions to conflicts. Consequently, we find ourselves in frantic pursuit of knowledge about strategic planning, computer technology, political systems and leadership styles. Also, we live constantly with the expectation that we can identify, address and resolve the "burning issues" of the moment, whether social, moral, political, educational or religious.

Nouwen is right. Such competence comes from the behavioral sciences which are frequently based upon secular and humanistic assumptions. So, Nouwen says, in our pursuit of relevance, we move farther and farther away from the mind and heart of Jesus Christ. The same feverish pursuit of relevance keeps us dancing on the hot coals of burning issues— whether to the left on nuclear arms, sexism, homosexuality and civil rights or toward the right on school prayer, pornography, crime, family and traditional values.

Ironically, Nouwen notes that the more we Christian leaders move toward competence and relevance, the more marginal we become. He brings us home with the question Jesus asked Peter three times after the Resurrection, "Do you love me?" With this question, Jesus lets us know that the first call upon the Christian leader is not competence or relevance, but embodiment of the Incarnational heart of Jesus Christ, which is characterized by unconditional love. This, in reality, is the unmatched competence and relevance we bring to our role as Christian leaders. To rely on any other source is to push us to the margins of the secular world and away from the heart of God.

But, to restate Nouwen's question, "How do we stay home?" The answer is through the discipline of contemplative prayer. Quite in contrast with our exhaustive activism, Nouwen calls us who are Christian leaders to the most difficult discipline of all—calm, quiet and reflective prayer.

The Resolution of Incarnate Community

To be a *vulnerable* Christian leader is equally difficult and demanding. Nouwen foresees the *"desire to be spectacular"* as the second temptation which Christian leaders of the future will face with mounting pressure. Not unlike Satan's challenge for Jesus to throw Himself down from the pinnacle of the temple and be rescued by angels, the nature of the media world creates in us a lust for the spectacular. But the bald truth is that we are continually trying to "raise the score" to call attention to ourselves. Nouwen's penetrating insight reminds us that we can only seek the spectacular when we fly solo. Thus, the temptation of the Christian leader is to draw farther and farther away from the mutuality, intimacy and accountability to the body of Christ.

Scores of books and thousands of words have been written in attempts to analyze the scandals, defections, burn-outs, failures and breakdowns among Christian leaders in recent years. With just a few words, Nouwen's Spirit-guided insight gives us the answer. By leaving Harvard University and entering Daybreak, a community for ministering to mentally handicapped people, he found himself under the constant need to minister and receive ministry. For the lectures at the

Center for Human Development, which became the text for his book *In the Name of Jesus*, he took Bill, one of the residents at Daybreak, with him. Bill sat next to the podium while Nouwen spoke, confirmed what he said with his own rambling commentary and, after hearing the commendations for the speech, added, "And we did it together, didn't we?" He answered, "Bill, thanks for coming with me. It was a wonderful trip and what we did, we did together—in Jesus' name."

Nouwen comes even closer to home when he confesses that it is harder for him to be faithful when he is alone. Accountability is a requirement for the Christian leader of the future which can only be achieved within the disciplines of confession and forgiveness that are exercised in the context of community. To be vulnerable, then, Nouwen concludes, "Christian leaders are called to live the Incarnation, that is, to live in the body—not only in their own bodies—but also in the corporate body of the community, and to discover there the presence of the Holy Spirit."[10] The challenge is to accept the full meaning of Jesus' instruction to Peter after the disciple avowed his unconditional love. "Feed my sheep" is the call to vulnerable leadership, ministering *to* others and receiving the ministry *of* others, as a confessing and forgiving member of the Body of Christ.

The Resolution of the Incarnate Word

To be a *trusting leader* is the third spiritual quality in Nouwen's profile for the Christian leader of the future. The temptation, he says, "is to be powerful." Just as Satan wooed Jesus with the wealth and power of all the kingdoms of the world under the guise of fulfilling his mission, Christian leaders know the same temptation. Although I contest Nouwen's classification of all power as carnal, I accept his definition when power is used as the leader's point of control. He comes too close for comfort. As the president of a college, university or seminary for almost thirty years now, I know the not-so-subtle need to be in control. In fact, I find myself on the verge

of panic when I cannot find the handle to solve a problem or
make a decision. When it happens, the temptation is to use
every available tactic of power to regain control.

With an insight into Scripture that I have never seen before, Nouwen cites the words of Jesus to Peter after His question, "Do you love me?" and His instruction, "Feed my sheep."
In a mystifying metaphor, Jesus reminds Peter:

> I tell you the truth,
> when you were younger
> you dressed yourself
> and went where you wanted;
> but when you are old
> you will stretch out your hands,
> and someone else will dress you
> and lead you where you do not want to go.
> John 21:18 NIV

Does Jesus mean that a Christian leader must give up control? Nouwen answers, "Yes," and I suspect he is so right that I
still do not want to admit it.

What an indictment upon all of us who must be in control
as Christian leaders! We have sought and exercised the power
of control—over people, money, time, space, information,
policy and procedure, and law—as our primary instrument
for advancing the gospel. No wonder Christianity is considered politically and economically powerful, but morally and
spiritually marginal in our society. Control, not trust, has
been our unspoken leadership goal. For this reason, Nouwen
sees the discipline of theological thinking as the means for
discerning where and how God is moving among people,
organizations and nations. Our greatest need for the future
is discerning Christian leaders who have given the control
over to God. At this point, Nouwen's tendency toward mysti-
cism lifts a bit. He poses the realities of human events to
which Christian leaders must speak prophetically—personal
struggles, family conflicts, national calamities and interna-

tional tensions. But no sooner are the issues posed than Nouwen returns to the Incarnational mode and drives the definition of "theology" back to its root meaning, which is none other than "thinking with the mind of Christ." To be a Christian leader, then, is to discern the signs of the times with the mind and under the control of Christ.

Profile of the Twenty-First Century Christian Leader

Can we reconcile the functional and spiritual qualifications for the twenty-first century Christian leader? By now, a paradox is not new. Whether Christian or secular, functional or spiritual, realistic or mystical—the tension between different worlds, roles and styles is not unlike the other conundrums that we have encountered. As Nouwen puts it, Christian leadership is identified as "downward mobility ending on a cross."[11] Of course! We must die to live, lose to gain and follow to lead. But from our cross, we are buried with Him in His death and raised with Him in the newness of His life—to embody His Spirit, embrace His vision and empower His people. Of course! To be a praying, vulnerable and trusting leader is first and foremost for our Incarnational character. But the spiritual disciplines of contemplative prayer, mutual ministry and theological thinking only release in us the energizing gift of the Holy Spirit to become:

. . . *Strategists for the redemptive vision* —initiating a global perspective which begins at home and taking the creative risks to "seek and save the lost";
. . . *Spokespersons for biblical truth*—discerning moral issues, making critical decisions and speaking the truth in love;
. . . *Servants of human need* —serving and being served as an accountable member of the corporate and communal "Body of Christ"; and

. . . *Stewards of spiritual power*—modeling the self-giving of death and discipline which inspires every follower to become an Incarnate leader.

Who will follow Him? Those of us who would lead must walk the path of downward mobility that ends on a cross. There, the paradox is resolved. Through the power of the Resurrection and the act of Incarnation, we rise to

. . . *embody* the character of Christ,
. . . *embrace* the vision of Christ and
. . . *empower* the people of Christ.

Who will follow Him? Those of us who would lead must do the disciplines of Christ which keep us focused, accountable and under His control. Then, by death and discipline, grace and gift, we will become effective Christian leaders for the twenty-first century—global in our vision, accountable in our servanthood and faithful in our stewardship. Breaking all the bounds of human expectation, the promise will be ours.

GREATER WORKS THAN THESE SHALL YOU DO!

Case in Point

Return to your thoughts about keynoting a national conference for emerging young leaders on the subject "Profile for the Twenty-first Century Christian Leader."

1. Would you change your introductory assumptions about the 1990s and the twenty-first century which bear directly upon the expectations for Christian leaders?

2. Would you change the qualifications in your profile? Which qualifications of Christian leadership would you add or subtract? Would you change the rank of those qualifications according to importance?

3. How would you include the dimensions of Incarnational leadership?

4. Would you change the distinguishing quality of a Christian leader or modify its emphasis?

5. Rethink the conclusion of your speech to spell out the meaning of Christ's promise, "Greater works than these shall you do." How do you want to see this promise fulfilled in your own leadership role?

Endnotes

Chapter 1

1. Walbert Buhlmann, *The Coming of the Third Church* (Marynoll, N.Y.: Orbis Books, 1972), 11–12.
2. Robert Bellah, *Habits of the Heart* (New York: Harper and Row, 1986), 41ff.

Chapter 2

1. Arthur Sharplin, *Strategic Movement* (New York: McGraw-Hill, Inc., 1985). The general format for the chart which also serves as reader's guide for the book is borrowed with credit and gratitude from Sharplin's book.

Chapter 3

1. Ibid., 149ff.
2. James MacGregor Burns, *Leadership* (New York: Harper and Row, 1978).

Chapter 4

1. Gary A. Yukl, *Leadership and Organizations* (Englewood Cliffs, N.J.: Prentice-Hall, 1981), 132.
2. Lee Iacocca, *Talking Straight* (New York: Harper and Row, 1988).

3. Jack Eckerd, *Eckerd: Finding the Right Prescription* (Old Tappan, N.J.: Fleming H. Revell Co., 1987), 179–180.

Chapter 6

1. C. S. Lewis, *Christian Reflections,* ed. Walter Hooper (Grand Rapids: W. B. Eerdmans Publishing Co., 1967), 7.

Chapter 7

1. Thomas J. Peters and Robert H. Waterman, *In Search of Excellence* (New York: Harper and Row, 1982), 26.
2. Henry Mintzberg, "The Strategic Concept I: Five P's for Strategy," *California Management Review* (Fall 1987) 11–32.
3. Warren Bennis and Burt Nanus, *Leaders: The Strategies for Taking Charge* (New York: Harper and Row, 1985), 29.
4. John Gardner, *No Easy Victories* (New York: Harper and Row Publishers, 1968), 32–33.
5. Bennis and Nanus, *Leaders,* 30.
6. Buhlmann, *Coming of the Third Church,* 3ff.

Chapter 8

1. Peters and Waterman, *Excellence,* 10–11.
2. Jonathan Koskol, *Rachel and Her Children* (New York: Crown Publishers, 1988), 39.
3. Bennis and Nanus, *Leaders,* 58ff.

Chapter 10

1. David L. McKenna, *Renewing Our Ministry* (Waco, TX: Word Books, 1986), 24ff.
2. Thomas J. Peters, "Symbols, Patterns and Settings: An Optimistic Case for Getting Things Done," Organizational Dynamics (Autumn 1978) AMACOM, A Division of American Management Associations.
3. Bennis and Nanus, *Leaders,* 37–38.
4. Nicholas Wolterstorff, *Educating for Responsible Action* (Grand Rapids: W. B. Eerdmans Publishing Co., 1980), 56–57.
5. James G. March and Michael D. Cohen, *Leadership and Ambiguity: The American College President* (New York: McGraw-Hill Book Co., 1974), 81ff.

6. Peters and Waterman, *Excellence*, 10–11.
7. Bennis and Nanus, *Leaders*, 72.

Chapter 11

1. Terence R. Mitchell and James R. Larson, Jr., *People in Organizations: An Introduction to Organizational Behavior*, third ed. (New York: McGraw-Hill Book Co.), 480.
2. Bennis and Nanus, *Leaders*, chapter 1.

Chapter 13

1. "The Twenty-First Century Executive," *U.S. News and World Report*, Vol. 104, No. 9 (March 7, 1988), 48ff.
2. Neil Chesanow, *The World Class Executive* (New York: Ranson Associates, 1985).
3. Frank Newman, *Higher Education and American Resurgence* (Princeton, N.J.: Carnegie Foundation for the Advancement of Teaching, 1985), xiii.
4. Koskol, *Rachel*, 63.
5. Edwin S. Gustad, *Faith of Our Fathers* (San Francisco: Harper and Row Publishers, 1987), 139.
6. Ibid.
7. Ibid., 136.
8. Ibid., 139.
9. Henri J. M. Nouwen, *In the Name of Jesus: Reflections on The Future of Christian Leadership* (Crossroads, N.Y., to be published 1989).
10. Ibid.
11. Ibid.